Beyond
Knowledge

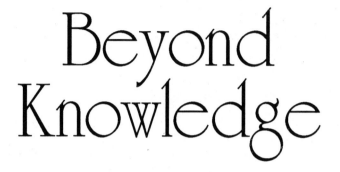

Beyond Knowledge

Jean Klein

Edited by Emma Edwards

▶◀ Third Millennium Publications
St. Peter Port • London • Santa Barbara

ISBN No. 1-877769-23-1

Library of Congress Catalog Card No. 93-061846

Design and production by Janet Andrews
Albion Studio, San Rafael, CA

Cover: Priest-King 1500 B.C. Fresco, Palace of Knossos, Courtesy of the Museum of Herakleion, Crete

JEAN KLEIN author of many books on non-dualism, Jean Klein spent several years in India going deeply into the subjects of Advaita and Yoga. Since 1960 he has been teaching and listening in Europe and the United States, engaging the attention of those who question their lives and yearn for insights into the real meaning of existence. He emphasizes the "Direct Way" to knowledge, without elaborate programs or practices.

Other Books by Jean Klein

Open to the Unknown (Third Millennium Publications, Guernsey)

Transmission of the Flame (Third Millennium Publications, Guernsey)

I Am (Third Millennium Publications, Guernsey)

The Ease of Being (Acorn Press, U.S.A.)

Be Who You Are (Element Books, England)

Who Am I? (Element Books, England)

Acknowledgments

DEEPEST THANKS to all those who helped bring this book to fruition, including Janet Andrews, Stephan Bodian, Mary Dresser, Channing Jones, Giorgos Mavrogiannis, Barbara Patterson, Pat Patterson, Vincenzo & Paula Santiglia, and Don Wetherly.

Preface

THIS BOOK, based on dialogues in Sounion, Greece, and London, England, in 1992 and 1993, is dedicated to the friends who came to these meetings and to all those who will come together through *sruti*, the truth.

It is not important to understand these words, but it is essential to live with the feeling they evoke. In living with their invocation, an inner ripeness grows. This maturity brings us to discover our silent being which is beyond knowledge.

Sounion, Greece

We have not come together to satisfy our intellects. This we can do through books and second-hand information. We have come to satisfy the inner need to know ourselves, to share our oneness, to hear directly what life is. To receive life we must be open to it. Life can only be understood by life. This means that the being open is itself life. During these meetings, be open to the openness, allow yourself to be deeply impregnated by the sayings which come directly from life. To be impregnated, the mind must be free from wrong knowing, that is, free from superimposing an independent existence on all that is objective. Nothing that can be known has existence in itself. It depends on a knower. The knower is consciousness. Only consciousness never changes. We must find out what never changes in us.

Have you any questions?

How can I be open to openness?
As long as you think there is something you are open to,

3

openness never comes. You will see that all that you try to become is only an object, but openness can never be an object. So, inquire in all directions until you come to the moment when there is nothing left to look for. Live this moment of silence. In this spontaneous giving up of objects, what remains is presence, where there is nobody present to anything.

I want very much to know myself, but I am afraid of this giving up of objects. I suppose I lack conviction that presence without objects is not a blank, bland state. Where does this lack of faith come from?
From memory. You only know yourself in objects, so you are open only to objects and have never allowed yourself to be permeated by unconditioned silence.

How can I know that this unconditioned silence is really full, desirable, not boring, something that I really want? How can I be convinced that I really want enlightenment?
You can only hear the teacher and ask how it is and how it can be attained. Of course, he will say it is not attainable. When you really hear this, it will have a deep impact on you. Live with this impact.

From your own experience, how would you describe the state of silence?
It is fullness, completeness. There is nothing to add or take away. It is ultimate contentment. It is a feeling that all is in its splendor without any need of alteration. You discover your own splendor and yourself in it. There is

no more "out there," no more objects. All is in glory, your glory.

So the fear of silence, the fear of committing myself totally to presence without objects, is a complete illusion?
Yes, it is ignorance based on the fear of disappearing. But there is nothing to disappear. In the feeling of fear you will discover a fear of dying. But when you discover life, you will see there is no death. So, first face life. Life is a continuum, there is no beginning and no end. Go very deeply in you and discover that which has never changed. You know the many changes in you, but the knower of these changes has never changed. I am not giving you answers. I stimulate questions.

Dr. Klein, what is life?
You can have a glimpse of it, but you cannot define it. You can only see what does *not* belong to life, what has no reality in itself, what is an expression of life but is not life itself. A phenomenal object has no existence in itself, it depends on consciousness, on awareness. Consciousness exists by itself, in itself. It does not need a perceiver. It is its own perceiving. It is in stillness that you discover life.

With which faculty do we glimpse life?
When you have discovered what is not life, you will automatically be life. The glimpse is with your totality. Your whole being is included. It does not go through the mind. It is not polluted by time and space. The mind

5

functions in direction. Thought is a contraction. When the brain is relaxed, it is multidimensional and open, open to the totality of being.

You said before, "Go deep inside you to discover that which does not change." Who goes deep? What is this going? And where is that depth?
There is nobody who goes deeply. There is only being the deep. You will be invited by it. The invitation comes from the invitee. The looker is what he is looking for. There is no duality. There is only one.

Dr. Klein, many times you use the expressions "to be available" and "to be open." I would like you, please, to explain a little more about this and if they are the same thing.
In the state of availability, you are relaxed, there is no anticipation, there is no end-gaining. In other words, you are waiting without waiting. In these moments of solicitation, this availability is not an object, so you do not emphasize what you are available to, but you emphasize the availability itself, the ultimate subject. It is It which is waiting for It.

Dr. Klein, I would like to know how creativity can be developed in us.
Look around you without thinking, without conceptualization. In seeing, come to no conclusion, no interpretation. Simply be in pure perception, pure seeing, pure looking, pure hearing, pure touching, and so on. At these moments you are free from memory and are open to the

unknown. You discover things that you never saw before. You see things from a completely new point of view—if we can still speak of a point of view since it is a global feeling. In pure observation, pure sensation, brain cells which are generally not used are completely open to the creative world. Creativity can never be thought, it comes to you. You must put yourself in a state of receiving, in a state of availability. Do not contaminate these moments with the already known. In other words be open to the unknown.

Coming back to the previous question, is there a difference between "being open" and "being available"?
When you find yourself in availability and openness, there is no difference. On a superficial level, when you are available for something, there may be tension. But when you are in this openness, the openness is absorbed in the openness. You are open to the openness. This openness can never become an object. Then you discover your real being, which is only availability, which is openness. There is nothing objective.

In this openness you find yourself adequate to every situation. There is no choice in this position, and you understand what is spontaneity. You are completely out of the vicious circle of pain and pleasure. The solution comes to you like an intuition, an apperception. When you are open, free from the past, creativity comes to you. It takes time to realize it in space and time, but the insight of this creativity is constantly present as a background.

Dr. Klein, does it in fact all depend on ourselves or our absence of self? It would seem that one needs to have the capacity to let go. On the other hand, things seem to be determined and one has to wait for something to happen that one cannot instigate by oneself.

In this state of which we are speaking, we live in intelligence. Nothing is impossible. It may be that you have to learn something or ask somebody for help who has the possibility to help you. There is no destiny. And there is no free will.

This is why I have come, to find someone from whom to learn.

You are in the right place.

[laughter]

Please, teach me.

I want to go back to the answer that you gave before about the fear of death and the fear of life. I am afraid of death. I am afraid of life. What can I do not to be afraid?

Who is afraid? Find out who it is. Is there really one who lives? In life, there is no place for an observer. Speaking of incarnation, who incarnates? These are questions one must live with.

What is afraid is not afraid. A concept is not afraid. Find out and explore the actual perception, the sensation of fear, where it is localized in your body, its density and so on. In discovering the percept you are disassociated from it. In exploring what *you* are not, you discover what you are.

So, in exploring a perception, for example, tension in the body, the goal is not really to have a relaxed body but to know the perceiver of the body?
Absolutely. That is the real goal. A body free from tension is a side effect of the exploration.

In doing the postures I find myself very often basking in the relaxed body or in a body sensation that is light and delicious.
That is an achievement. One must see that the goal is not the body. The goal is the owner of the body. Ask yourself, "Where is the perceiver?" The good body feeling is only a fraction of this art of yoga.

When one asks, "Where is the perceiver?" is it not the same question as "Who am I?" which we ask at every moment in a kind of regression ad infinitum?
Yes, absolutely, and you will discover in the end that there is no "who." The question is the answer. The highest answer is negative. The moment you make it positive you make an object of it.

So, if I feel I need to do something every day, the postures or breathing, and my day is not complete without it, does this mean I am emphasizing the object?
Yes, absolutely.

In Indian philosophy, it is said that we choose our incarnation and our parents and the situations in which we live.
It all belongs to the romanticism of India. [laughter] You

cannot chase away these questions like that. Ask very seriously: Who lives? You will never find him. There is no entity who lives. There is only living.

Since individuality is an illusion, then it makes sense that there is no free will and no predetermination, because these are in reference to an individuality.
Absolutely. Did you ask to be born? Will you ask to die? Have you asked for the suffering that you have? Where is your free will?

I see that I have no free will, but that is my destiny.
There is no destiny because there is no person to be destined. As long as you believe you are an individual entity, there is destiny. But this belief is an illusion. In reality there is no person, no karma and no destiny.

...However, is there not predetermination with respect to the body, where it is born, where it dies, what happens to it, what it looks like, etc.?
The body is energy in movement. One day, all that is composed as body will join the global energy. But presence, consciousness, has not been born, and what has not been born cannot die. The tool, the body, is conditioned by language, heredity, father, mother. It is a machine like any other machine. It asks for proper food to maintain it in the right way. When you are free from the one who lives, there is only living, and that way of living is joyful. The moment you create a "liver," there is choice, and where there is choice there is conflict.

If one is free from individuality, then could there still be a script or a film for the body?
The body is conditioned. Conditioning is in the film, but the knower of the conditioning is not in the film.

Then this conditioning is predetermined?
To have an answer, you must live with the question: How can I become free from all conditioning? Of course, the body and mind are, to an extent, conditioned by race, glands, culture, and so on. But you are not the body-mind, so don't fight this biological conditioning. Simply see how you react in the moment itself. What you are is beyond conditioning.

Does what you said about the body include the mind or does the mind work separately?
The body is an expression of life, an extension of life; it is perceived in space and time. It needs a perceiver, it needs consciousness to be known. It has no reality of its own. When you see it in a right way, it is perceived by consciousness in consciousness; it is nothing other than consciousness.

What is the relationship between energy, which is floating around, and consciousness? Consciousness is aware of energy, but then what is energy?
Energy is not consciousness. Consciousness has no quality. Energy is an extension, an expression of consciousness. But consciousness is not affected by this expression. Consciousness is, but does not exist in space and time.

11

Is consciousness the background onto which time and space are superimposed?
Yes.

In your books you mention a "geometrical representation." What do you mean by this? Is it an essential element in understanding, and, if so, how can one come to it?
It is better to come to the geometrical understanding before it dissolves in being understanding. It gives clarity to the mind.

Does it mean that one understands the truth in the mind in some way?
Yes, it is transposition on the mental level. You see the truth in one moment before it dissolves in being.

How will I know when I have a clear geometrical representation?
Because it is clarity. Because it does not keep you on its phenomenal level. The mind is freed. When the deepest urge to be the ultimate is there, the residues of the phenomenal dissolve.

The word "geometrical" for most people seems complicated, yet you say that being truth is simple. Why do you use this mathematical expression?
Because in my life it appeared in this way.

Because you have a mathematical mind?
Yes, but it may appear differently to another. We should

not emphasize the word geometrical. It is an inner perspective of the truth.

Can the geometrical understanding, if it is phenomenal, be built up gradually?
Not exactly, because it comes through insight, not through the linear mind. You may have several insights, then in one moment a whole representation of the truth appears and the mind is at once freed from wrong thinking. Then the representation dissolves in being.

Once the whole picture is clear in a flash, does it necessarily dissolve in being?
Yes, if the ultimate desire is there, because it points directly to the ultimate.

You said it is "better" to come to a geometrical understanding before being understanding. Can one come directly to being understanding?
Yes, but it will not be completely integrated. One must, in any case, go beyond the phenomenal.

Dr. Klein, speaking of the phenomenal, is it possible for you to talk about what is proper to eat?
The body is the result of what has been absorbed. One can give certain ideas of proper nourishment, but mainly one must observe for oneself: How do you feel before taking food? How do you feel after taking food? How do you go to sleep? How is your sleep? How is your waking up? Food is not only what you absorb by mouth. Food

is your feeling and your thinking and your acting, too. But I think one should eat living food, and cooked food is not alive any more. Certain foods should be cooked to a degree, I agree. It also depends on what one does with one's life, one's activity. In your case, as you are a doctor and you receive patients in the morning, it is better not to eat heavy food because it calls for great sensitivity and clear perception to see clearly with whom you are dealing. But the most important thing is to observe how you wake up in the morning. Before the body wakes up you should be full of joy. Otherwise you are ill. But do not go to the hospital! How you wake up in the morning is very important. It depends on how you go to sleep.

Dr. Klein, could you say more about how it is possible to wake up in joy?
Before going to sleep, one should put away all the qualifications of oneself, all kinds of affectivity. One should find oneself completely naked. When you go to sleep in this way, there is a certain waking up before the body wakes up. This joy is not in space and time. It can be one moment. But in this moment, I would say there is eternity. It is joy free from all psychological experiences.

So there is a waking up before the body wakes up, one is not awake all the time?
In deep sleep you are the light, but you are not awake in the light. There is a moment's transition where you are awake in the light but not in the body.

In which faculty is this awakening felt?
In the subtle body, the subtle brain.

*Does this waking up feel as though one is simply in aware-
ness without any sense perception?*
Yes, exactly. You are not awake in objects.

*The joy, the awareness, is not in time and space, but the
moment of awakening is in time and space?*
It is duration, but there is no knower to perceive it. Later,
the body-mind automatically wakes up.

Can anything be done to sustain the moment?
One cannot prolong it in the moment itself because there
is no one present. You cannot think of the present. You
can only be it. That means it is not in subject-object
relationship. There is no observer and something observed. It is your non-dual reality.

But you can live with it during the day, be solicited
by it, let it remain the background to your waking state.

*Is the moment of being awake in light, while the senses are
absent, the same as the dying process, what is sometimes
called "dying in the light"?*
Yes. When you have once experienced dying to all that
is, in other words, being awake in the absence of objects,
the process of dying is a spontaneous giving up.

What is divine judgment?
When the self passes away, there is no punishment.

Saying that there is punishment after we pass away is simply satanic. Our society must not punish. We must help people to change. How we make them conscious of what they have done depends on the society. But in a society which is really ripe, there is no punishment. We have not been authorized to punish, because we are all still responsible for all that appears in this society.

Where does suffering come from?
When you live in choice you are in the cycle of pleasure and pain. As long as you live in this vicious circle, you will suffer. It seems that the joy is very short and the suffering is very long. But it is only because you identify with the experience in space and time that your suffering seems long and your joy short. The moment you are free from the person, you are out of the circle.

Look deeply into what is meant by "volition without volition," volition without interference by the "I-concept." It is not the person who wills an action, but the situation which "wills" it. The "I," the "me," is in constant choice, because you identify with what is security for you and avoid what is insecure. Pain and pleasure come together like two sides of a coin. You cannot have one without the other.

When we go to a museum and look at a beautiful painting or when we listen to a beautiful piece of music, is this pleasure?
It is not pleasure. For me, pleasure is degenerated joy. When you see a painting, first you have a sudden im-

pact—without knowing why—that it is beautiful. It gives you joy. It takes you beyond. Then you come back to see why and analyze the qualities of the painting. Pleasure for the senses comes in the analysis. The canvas is not itself joyful, it is you who superimpose joy on the painting. The real joy comes after the seeing.

So many philosophies talks about pleasure and pain, and it seems as though the way to avoid pain is to avoid pleasure and you have a monotonous, flat life and that's why I am interested in understanding more about this experience of looking at beautiful art, beautiful music.
We can only see beauty outside when we have beauty in us. We superimpose our own beauty on an object. Our real nature is beauty. It is inherent in the nature of the painter, sculptor or poet, who live from time to time in this beauty, to share it with their surroundings. We must love our own beauty, this beauty which is causeless. We are very often solicited by this beauty, but we live too much in projection of psychological beauty, which is completely opposed to the causeless beauty of which we are speaking.

I cannot in myself distinguish psychological beauty from the causeless beauty that you talk about.
Psychological beauty represents itself every time there is an object; it is a subject-object relationship. The causeless beauty of which we are speaking is objectless. It is you. You are It. When you live it, you live in another way. Objectless joy is what you experience without an

experiencer, in love. The joy that you live in love can never be found in a subject-object relationship that needs an observer and a thing observed.

Dr. Klein, would you please talk about perception and exactly what you mean when you say that we must be open to pain? To accepting pain?
The non-accepting of the pain contributes to the pain.

I don't understand very well what it means to accept the pain. How do I do it?
It is not a fatalistic way of accepting. It is not a masochistic succumbing to the pain. It is passive-active, with a view to knowing something about the pain. The knower of the pain has nothing to do with the pain. When you feel this strongly, then you are distanced from the object, pain, and it is no longer painful. As long as you live in the "concept," pain, you cannot face the percept. So to come to the percept, first free yourself from the concept. The concept "pain" is not painful.

I don't quite understand what it is to accept, how to do it, how can I be free of the pain, how can I change the pain into

a stream of energy?
You know your pain through your reactions on the body level. When you look at how you function, you will see that you stay for a very short time with the perception of the pain because you immediately conceptualize it. And as the perception and the conception can never happen simultaneously, the moment you conceptualize you lose contact with the perception. So now the question is, how to face what you conceptualize as "pain." You must go back to the body level. See where the pain is localized, explore the localization. Simply take note of it without interpreting it as "pain." In doing so you will experience space between the knower and the known, and you become free of the identification with the pain.

This is what I was trying to find out: Do you mean to detach myself from the pain and to look at it simply as an observer?
Yes. When you see it as a fact, there is space between the observer and the observed. And then comes a very important observation: You will see that the pain is in you, but you are not in the pain.

Thank you very much.
In this way, pain is a pointer. It points to where the knower of the pain knows itself, the ultimate self. So do not take your pain as a punishment coming from somewhere. But find out where it points. It points to your real nature.

Can we also talk about perception?

The perceived is an object, but the perceiver can never be objectified. Remain in pure perception, free from any thinking, from any reasoning, free from the concept.

Dr. Klein, in a dialogue of Krishna Menon's, he recognized that not all people readily come to silence by means of meditation, and he suggested there was another way by constantly referring the thoughts, of whatever quality they might be, back to the consciousness from which they arise. Can you say more of this, because it was not all that clear how that might take place.

All happens in consciousness, all is perceived by consciousness. Menon meant: Bring the seen back to the seeing, bring the heard back to the hearing. Because the heard and the perceived have their being in the hearing and the seeing. The seen has its potentiality in the seeing. There is no seen without seeing. Nothing seen can exist out of seeing. So it means: When you face the perceived, the perceived is an expression of consciousness. So bring the perceived back to the perceiving. The perceiver, the hearer, can never be an object, perceived nor heard. It is objectless. It is consciousness. This is what Krishna Menon meant. It is very difficult to explain. You would ask now, how can you bring the seen back to the seeing and the heard back to the hearing? When the heard and the seen have unfolded completely, when the object perceived or heard has given up all its secret to you, then automatically it comes back to its homeground. It has its homeground in consciousness. But this consciousness you can never objectify, because you are it. It is a global feeling of completeness. But it is one way. There are other ways also.

Every object has a mission to bring us back to its homeground. The object has only two missions: one mission is to reveal the ultimate, and the second is to glorify the ultimate in many ways.

What is it in us that allows for the unfolding?
When the subject is fixed on the object, the body is in a state of tension. In the unfolding of the object, the body comes to a great letting go. It is only in deep relaxation that the object can dissolve in the subject. We must be completely available to all the possibilities of the object, free from choice, selection, interpretation, and so on. We must not grasp it but receive it with all our body sensitivity. When we do not direct the object, it unfolds in our multidimensional attention.

Is being available a passive or active relaxed state?
It is open, actively relaxed. In passive relaxation you are open to objects. In active relaxation you are open to the self.

So in exploring a perception, should one be first passively receptive?
Yes, let the object come to you. Then there is a kind of switchover where you go from passive to active availability, and finally this dissolves and what remains is only consciousness.

Dr. Klein, yesterday you suggested that there was no such thing as divine punishment. If ideas like Day of Judgment, Heaven and Hell are just in the mind, then why is this form of teaching used in certain religious traditions?
It is only to stop the simple-minded from acting in ways that could disrupt society. In reality, there is nobody to be punished and there is no entity in the cosmos to punish.

If there is no punishment, how can we deal with serious criminals?
Of course the criminal must be separated from the society. But not with the primary intention to punish. Society must protect itself, but at the same time, see whether the ill person is recoverable. Society is responsible for its own crimes.

Dr. Klein, could you please tell us what is the role that the personality has to play?
Only in the absence of the personal presence is there a place for the ultimate presence. You must see that the personal presence has no reality. In this personal presence there is no place for the ultimate presence. The personal presence is in space and time, but the presence of which we are speaking is timeless. It is only this presence which is in the now.

The personality is a very useful tool with which to face the phenomenal world. It is simply like your car or house. To identify yourself with your car or your house seems unacceptable. Yet you do not clearly see the unac-

ceptability of identifying with the personality. This identification goes very deep because you spend all your
efforts trying to be free from it in one way or another.
One day you will see that the one who tries to free himself
from the prison of this identification, the "liberator," also
belongs to the prison. When you see you are in a prison,
that the prisoner, in all his efforts to escape, belongs to
the prison, in this moment you are out of the process,
free from the prison. And then I would say: Be it, be the
freedom. You will realize that in reality you were never
in prison and so there is no meaning in trying to get out.

When you need the personality, it comes to you. It is
the situation which asks for it. But it is a completely
transparent personality. You need it, you use it, and you
forget it. There is no memory in it. Identifying with the
personality must come to an end, and in this absence
there is presence. The personality is psychological memory. How can you face life through memory? Life never
repeats; it is always new. It is only psychological memory
that maintains the "I-concept." In living free from memory there is spontaneity, and in this spontaneity you are
completely adequate to every situation.

*Yesterday we were talking about matter and energy and I
am not clear as to what energy is exactly. Is it something to
do with St. John's "in the beginning was the Word"?*
In the beginning was the Word. Goethe said in the
beginning was action, doing. For action and for doing,
for pronouncing, of course you need energy. All that is
perceived is matter, is energy in movement. Conscious-

ness is not limited to energy. Energy is in consciousness.
When you say to yourself "I am," there is no energy.
Because the pronoun "I" can never be objectified, never
thought. The "I Am" points to your deepest nature.

How can we face everyday violence?
Be aware that you are violent with yourself. Do not say,
"I am not violent." When you face violence with reaction,
you are an accomplice to the violence. You must face it
free from reaction; then there will be the intelligence to
act, or not act, appropriately.

Dr. Klein, if there is no "I," what is the real nature of desire?
It belongs to the body-mind tool. But the real desire in
us is to realize ultimate contentment. The forefeeling, the
taste of this contentment, comes out of the experience of
deep sleep without dreaming. Without the experience of
deep sleep, we would never conceive what is ultimate
happiness. And this ultimate happiness is our background, to use a geometrical analogy. It is constant
presence, it is a continuum. All that appears in space and
time moves in this continuity. It is certainly what you are
looking for.

*Does all desire come from the desire for contentment, or only
spiritual desire?*
All desire comes from the desire for contentment, but the
desire for a car or a house or a man or woman is a lack
of discrimination, a lack of seeing that objects can never
bring you to the end of desire. An object feeds another

object. When you inquire in yourself, all you desire is desirelessness. Objects are compensation, compensation for not feeling fulfilled.

Why is desire regarded as sinful or wrong in almost all religious traditions?
Because in the end the object brings conflict. It brings you nowhere.

Dr. Klein, you used the phrase a minute ago, "use the personality as a tool" or words to that effect. My question: Who uses the personality? If it is the ultimate self, does the ultimate self do anything?
This personality is a packet of beliefs, second-hand information, experiences with which you identify yourself and say, "I am this." All that you perceive in daily life goes through this personality. When you see how the personality is really formed, you will use it in another way. It needs some deep inquiring to come to the understanding that there is not a doer, that there is not a thinker. There is no independent entity in the cosmos. Many books have been written, but no one has written a book. There is nothing personal. It needs a certain maturity to understand this.

Dr. Klein, when you say "when you see what the personality is composed of, when you see what it is made of, you will use the personality in a different way," who is the "you" that you are referring to?
You will not use it personally, because there is nothing

personal. This tool is really adequate to every situation. It is a useful instrument; otherwise, you use it for war.

There is no "you" really that is using the personality.
No. It is the situation that asks for the right tool, for the right acting, the right doing. You know yourself that at least eighty percent of our acting is through beliefs and second-hand information which we never question. When you do deeply in you, you will see that the desire behind desire is to be free from objects, free from the personal. In freedom from the person, there is beauty in living. But, see how you function in daily life.

What is the reason that we do not question our beliefs, our way of living? Isn't it because we often simply have no time for self-inquiry and is it not true that to be an inquirer one needs a certain period of freedom from worldly commitments?
One does not question the already known because there is a fear of facing the unknown. To give up what you know and face something new is very hard for many people. They would prefer to live in catastrophe.

A truth-seeker needs moments of stillness where the brain is open. An encumbered brain is not ready, not creative.

Is there a way that we can have consciousness in our deep sleep?
In deep sleep there is not a knower of the deep sleep; otherwise, it is not deep sleep. During deep sleep our

body is completely impregnated with felicity and beauty and peace. When we come to know how to go to sleep, we will, in the morning before the body wakes up, feel all the residues of this peace and beauty. All this desire for beauty and happiness comes from the experience of deep sleep. The desire to meditate comes only from this experience.

Is not deep sleep a state within consciousness rather than one being able to be conscious in deep sleep, as our friend says?
Yes, you go in and out of sleep. It is a state.

Would you please say a little bit more about the way to go to sleep?
During the day we are more or less constantly in defense, in reaction, in affectivity. So we must learn the art of giving all this up before going to sleep. This giving up is first on the level of the body, as we did this morning. We should give up all qualifications and find ourselves in complete nakedness. This nakedness is the preparation for a completely new waking up. Waking up is, of course, in space and time, but there is a moment before we create the world, before we create our body, which has nothing to do with space and time. It is a moment when we have, I would say, a glimpse of what has passed in deep sleep. This glimpse belongs most profoundly to us. Live with it in the morning, in the afternoon. This glimpse is not objective; it does not belong to the senses. One cannot find a reference to talk about it. It is not like describing

a mango where you can say it is not an apricot or a banana, and so on. There is no reference for this insight.

Generally, when we say we slept very well, we are referring to the body. But the extreme release from effort we feel on the body level is more or less a residue of the deep sleep. Take note of it. The mind must be informed that there is something beyond the mind. That is enough.

How do we create the body?
It is an object perceived.

Is our perceiving and creating the same?
Yes. We create according to our perception. I would even say, according to our need.

To the conditioned mind there is a conditioned creation and to the unconditioned mind, creation appears in its original state.
Yes, you see the whole, not fractions.

Just a confirmation. In answer to the question, "Who uses the personality?", was the answer that the circumstances use it?
Yes, there is not a user, there is only using.

It is used by the circumstances of life?
Yes, it is using without a user, if we can speak in this way. When you drive your car, there is only driving. If you think, "I am driving," you may have an accident. There is only doing in the doing.

29

When you talked about a personality that does not come from memory, you called it a "transparent" personality. Are there different transparent personalities?

Talking of different personalities implies many entities on the level of psychology, but there is nothing personal in the personality. The transparent personality is a collection of talents that come together when needed, then dissolve into non-personal consciousness.

When you listen, are open, to situations, the so-called personality functions in a different way. It is not really a *personality*. Nothing is personal; there is only listening to the situation, taking note of the fact, and acting. When there is no choice, where is the personality?

Can we enjoy for a few minutes the timeless moment?

Dr. Klein, last summer in answer to a question from me, you told me, "Follow beauty." I have kept these words inside me, trying not to work them with the mind, but I would like some more help, please.

Beauty cannot be objectified. It is. Look in you profoundly at what is beauty and you will discover that it is what has never changed in you. The love that you have for nature, for human beings, has never changed. Give all your intelligence, all your attention to it. You will be solicited very often by your own beauty. Be in identity with these moments. It is the only way. You must discover in yourself what is beauty.

I would like, if possible, to hear something about hope.

As long as you do not live knowingly in love, in beauty, there is hope. Hope is anticipation. There can only be hope for something. Hope exists when there is representation. When you have a forefeeling, an insight, hope comes to you from what you hope, from the fulfillment glimpsed in the insight. The average man has thousands of different hopes because he lives in becoming and memory. Hope disappears when you really face the present.

Hope would seem to be an obstacle to living in waiting without waiting.
Absolutely. When there is a glimpse of truth, hope disappears and you live in openness, in presence.

So, is hope like desire, when it is oriented to the ultimate it finds its real significance, otherwise it jumps from one thing to the next?
In real hope you face the hope itself and not the object. In this innocent hope there is no representation and no expecting.

Does every ego have to go through what St. John of the Cross calls "the dark night of the Soul" before it can give itself up?
You are not obliged to go through this darkness, because darkness does not lead to light. But the dark night may bring clarity if the ego is reduced. For example, you are in a dark room all your life and suddenly there is a ray of light. It may cause great suffering when you suddenly feel the darkness, the weight of the ego. You foresee the giving up, but you still see it in relation to the ego. If you saw it with global vision, there would be no suffering. Clarity is your real nature.

I would like to ask how we can activate our intuition, our insight.

Live with your question. Live very seriously with the sayings of the teacher. Do not try to make them understood. Let them be understanding. You will have an insight, but there is no way to go to it, and nobody to go there. You can only be open to it, available to it.

A little while ago you said that "the love you have for nature, for human beings, has never changed." I find it much easier to unconditionally love nature and animals than human beings, except very young children, because animals and nature and very young children are innocent and not devious like human beings. Can you comment?
It is true that it takes more maturity to love human beings, to know that they are one with you.

But that is an intellectual fact for me. It does not change the heart. Should one try to love one's neighbor as Christianity preaches?
Find out in your silence what you love in you. When this love is really alive you will feel it in others because it is not personal, it is an essence in common with all human beings.

How can I get beyond all the unlovable things in the personality to come to what is most lovable?
First you must believe what I say to you, that you are lovable. Then, like a scientist, follow my advice, the same advice that I followed to know that you are lovable! Discover that you are not your body, senses and mind, but something beyond. When you have inquired into the

body, senses and mind, there comes a point when there is no more to inquiry and you feel yourself directionless, at a living point from which all direction flows. You will find yourself in identity with it. It remembers you from time to time. Be this moment. It is without object, without any quality. It will be your companion all your life.

You have talked to us about the relation between art and truth. Can an actress find the way to truth through her profession of acting?
If you have a non-objective relationship with yourself and inquire what happens in you, you will also have an impersonal or non-objective relationship with the personage which you are playing on stage. You can never understand the person which you interpret on stage through your own person. When you are free from your own person, you are open to all the possibilities of interpretation. Then you must live with the personage. Come to the right pronunciation. It is in the pronunciation that you will find all the subtlety.

But I find it essential to draw on my experiences, my reactions, my personality, to build a part. Without any experience or background or memory, how can one feel empathy with the role?
Of course you use what is at your disposal to interpret. The interpreter must be absent first and then the elements of the role will come to you. It is in action that the actor appears.

You are passive-active?
Yes.

Could you please tell us how we can free ourselves from a habit, for example, smoking? Thank you.
It is mainly a reflex. Be aware every moment when this reflex appears to you. See that it is reflex. At that moment do not refuse the reflex; accept it. But you do not need to smoke a whole cigarette seven centimeters long. Smoke only half of it. Cut it in half. When you have once become aware of this reflex, you will become aware in other moments of other reflexes.

Do you mean to observe what I am doing?
Absolutely. It is the only thing that frees you from the reflex, and smoking is only a reflex. There may be some substance in it that you may need for a short time, but it is mainly a crutch that you need. The cigarette is a compensation. It helps you to feel that you look relaxed. What is important is that you become aware that it is a compensatory reflex. Simply take note of it. When you really take note of it, see what happens.

Could we say the same about all drugs?
Absolutely. Smoking, alcohol, narcotics, it is all a compensation.

For what exactly?
For what you most profoundly desire: harmony and freedom. When you feel stuck in your life, you feel

yourself bound and you try to escape with alcohol or other drugs.

Not on the same subject, I would like to ask about meditation. Like many other people, I have been taught meditation with a mantram. I would like to ask if this kind of meditation is positive or useful.

The mantram is chosen for the beautiful sound, for the beautiful vibrations in the pronouncing of the mantram. The mantram is not to be interpreted conceptually. It really only has a virtue through the sound. Our body is made up of many organs and each organ responds to the vibrations of certain sounds. So the right sound can bring you to a certain relaxation, quietness. But the relaxation of the body-mind can become a habit which keeps you in the subject-object relationship. When it becomes a habit, the mind can never be creative.

It is clear that the desire to meditate comes from the experience of deep sleep, which is a continuum free from space and time. Meditation is not a function, it is not an activity. It is a way of being where the brain is completely open. That is why when you live with certain deep questions with the mind in openness, in innocence, without expecting an answer, an unexpected answer comes up, because your brain is open to the unexpectable. Only in an unfurnished mind can creativity take place. This open mind is meditation.

As long as you think there is still someone to meditate, then continue to meditate. Keep looking for the meditator. You will never find him. The meditator is only a thought-construct. When this strikes you and you see that there is no one to meditate and nothing to meditate on, then you will automatically be in meditation.

Wait to be invited to meditate. Wait for the invitation, for the solicitation. It must not become a habit. What is important is that you meditate in activity. You must meditate with open eyes, open ears, open nostrils; otherwise, it is not meditation.

In meditation, is the mind still?
Yes. It is in its primordial state. When you see that you can only meditate on what you know already and you turn in a vicious circle of the known, you will come to a moment when there is no more activity, there is only stillness. It is this stillness which is the background of all appearance. It is absolutely free from space and time. In this stillness there is nobody still and nothing is still. You live then in identity with this stillness.

Make it also clear that in perceiving there is only perceiving. You cannot have a percept and a concept at the same time. *Alors*, keep yourself completely attuned with the perception. When you keep yourself completely with the perception, you are free from all parasites of thinking.

Dr. Klein, if I can return to the subject of acting. When you are playing a part on stage and you are living the part, you shed everything that is not in you; the part is in you, and your awareness includes the other actors, the inner life of the character, the audience. When you finish, the ego claims.

What can be done to prevent that?
First, you read the play that has been proposed. Then the second time you read the play, the relations between the different characters in the play will be clearer. Then you must bring the character you have chosen into relation with the others. So what now is important is improvisation. It is only when you improvise that you and the other actors can see whether there is real understanding of the role. According to the spontaneity and facility of the improvisation we can see if the play is ready. It is only in this interpretation that you will find all you need to express the part, the right body movements, the right emotions, the right voice. Realize that you do not play alone. You are not bound to the text. So free yourself from the text. Go to the text only at the end. Otherwise, you are bound to the text.

The day before yesterday we talked about maturity, ripeness. The usual meaning of the word, as I understand it, includes the notions of time and experience. But it seems that you are not using the word in this way. Can you say more about what you mean by this expression?
It is through inquiring without conclusion that maturity comes. Question situations, question life without any conclusion or solution. Then you will come to the unexpected. By maturity, I mean being ripe for understanding. Maturity can only come when you ask, "What is life?" It is the ripeness in you which brings you to the right formulation, "Who am I?", "What is life?" The answer comes only to a worthy person.

How would you describe the right formulation of "Who am I?" Is it a thought, a feeling, a sensation, an insight or a psychological inquiry?
The right formulation is beyond thought, but one must go through thought first to come to the question beyond it. It is a living question.

Dr. Klein, you have spoken of the personality as a tool and yet it seems that this tool is capable of loving, especially the love of mankind. When we see the society getting more violent and the personality getting more violent in accordance with the situation, does the personality need changing or the society?
The personality can never change society. The personality is a useful tool, but one must not use it personally. Take away all that is personal in the personality, and when you are not bound to it, not identified with it, it is a useful tool. It does not hinder you to be a lover or an admirer.

Does that mean that there is no such thing as humanity?
Free from identification with the personality there is no longer an ego, there is no longer an "I-concept." In the absence of the "I-concept" you may realize what you are profoundly. In the absence of the person, there is presence. It is only in the absence of yourself that there is presence. And then there is no relationship from object to object, from personality to personality. This is the real essence of our humanity. The relation between two personalities is only asking for security, help, being

loved, being recognized.

Does that then mean, sir, that the salvation of the individual is the salvation of humanity?
In the disappearance of the "I-concept" the relation between human beings will be in love.

Will it always be so?
I cannot give you a certificate.

I ask this because obviously you see the world and the creation in a very different way to the way I am seeing it. Yet, I am arrogant enough to think I am a happy person and I find it difficult to share this happiness with others.
Explore in you what is lovable and give all your intelligence and capacity to what is lovable in you. What is lovable in you is also lovable in the other one. And it is not objective. To really love another, you must first love yourself—but not what you ordinarily call yourself—because this self is the self of all.

I do not want to have negative feelings towards my husband. I have worked on this a lot and I do not know why there is this situation.
You must first find a teacher who will teach you. Love the teacher, not the teacher as a person, but the love in which he is established. When you find love in yourself, you will be ready to find the ultimate husband. I do not remember the exact formulation in the *Upanishads* [*Brhad Aranyaka*], "Love your wife not because she is

your wife; love your wife because God is in her." Do not emphasize the objective part, the externals, in your husband, but emphasize the love in him that you have in common with him.

You have said that the question is the answer. Could you speak a little more about that?
What is important in your life is to realize that the asker is the answer. There are not two. The seeker *est le trouvé* [is the found]. In the split mind one speaks of subject and object, but in action, where is the subject and where is the object? When you ask profoundly, in your absolutely relaxed state, "Who am I?", who is the asker? You can never find him. Then all comes to a stop. It is at this moment that you realize that the asker is the answer.

We have talked today and on previous days about personality and about the need for the personality to be devoid of the personal, if it is to be a useful tool. If, in facing a situation, we put aside the "I like, I don't like," would that aim be attained?
Absolutely. All that you have acquired—knowledge—is useful for you, but you should not use it in a personal way. When you use it in a personal way there is constantly choice, and you then live in the vicious circle of the pain and pleasure structure. So refer nothing to youself and yourself to nothing. Then you are completely available. Then you look at your life and the situations around you from your wholeness, from your globality, from your availability. In looking at a situation without

any comparison, volition is no longer personal, action is not reaction, as most of our actions are. And suddenly you see things that you never saw before when your looking was fractional. When there is choice in a situation, you know you are looking from the "I-concept." Your fractional view is missing many elements in the surroundings which belong to the present moment. You have experienced this: moments when you were in great conflict and one day, perhaps years later, you accidentally see the situation much more globally, and you see clearly what created the conflict.

There may be many moments when you spontaneously see globally and a conclusion presents itself, yet it is not you who comes to this conclusion. But you question the conclusion because it is not very pleasant for you at the time. When a conclusion comes spontaneously we should never let the ego put it into question.

There are moments when the heart opens up, and in those moments there is peace, there is love for whatever comes into one's perception. Then the personality interferes with such strength that its presence is judged to be undesirable. This seems to be a vicious circle that causes pain. How can one resolve this situation?

Of course, we are not fixed to one personality, we have thousands and thousands of possibilities. Free yourself from the object and remain only with the feeling of love. Bring every situation back to its background. Do not fight the ego, do not fight the controller. Refer all to the "I am," to all that is lovable in you. One day you will find yourself no longer in this discontinuity, but in the continuum which is constant, which is eternal. *You* never change.

The world appears to you according to the position which you have taken. From the point of view of the body, all belongs to the senses; from the mind, all belongs to affectivity. But from the point of view, which is not a point of view, of consciousness, there is no problem. It is very important to see that we create the problem through our own position.

But is there not a choice in this situation? In a way we have chosen our position and can choose whether or not to change it, can we not?
All the change that we can do is relative. Most people emphasize the faculty of sight when looking at the world. This is fractional. It is very interesting to look from different perspectives, touch, smell, hearing and so on. But we cannot choose to look from the ultimate because the mind cannot bring about this change. We can only be open to the choiceless. We can see that we look through choice, that we are not in global, choiceless looking.

Are there any questions?

Dr. Klein, earlier this week you directed our meditation together and you talked about the breath and the exhalation of the breath. Could you say more about the breath and meditation?

Inhalation and exhalation are more or less superimpositions on what is constant. So the silence, the interval after exhalation, is not an absence of activity but an absence of function. It is presence. In the beginning, our awareness focuses on the act of inhalation and exhalation. But there comes a moment that we become indifferent to inhaling and exhaling. It is now that the body takes itself in charge concerning the breathing, and we emphasize the silence, the interval between the two activities. That is a spiritual way of using breath control and breath itself, but breath control can also be used to direct, to orchestrate, the energy in us. I prefer the first way of dealing with the breathing.

Could you please talk about naming? At which point of the process of perception does naming come in, and is there a pure naming and a naming burdened by psychological intervention?

Naming is a natural brain function; it belongs to our culture. So an "elephant" is not a "mouse." But the moment evaluation, comparison, justification, comes in, then we are no longer in observation. We should cultivate pure observation without qualification.

This morning, in the yoga, you reminded us to be in the sensation and not to think. In one of the asanas the knees were painful and I tried just to give attention to the asana. Does the localized sensation become global? It did not happen to me.

When there is reaction in a certain part of the body, you should sense it. In sensing it, the reaction, the resistance, is absorbed by the sensation. In other words the localization is dispersed in the sensing. We can start by sensing the whole posture and the area around the contraction, or we can face the fraction first. In the latter case, we sense the contracted object part of the body and gradually the accent is released from the object until there is a sudden shift to the accent on awareness. Experience will tell you which is the correct way to face tension. We should sense every reaction. It is a tuning as you tune a cello or a piano. You must take your body for a harp.

This procedure in the postures can also be transposed onto the level of the mind. You become aware that you live constantly in anticipation, in end-gaining. In the body exercises we live really in the now, from moment to moment, fraction to fraction. At each moment the goal is attained.

Could you say something about visualization? I find it difficult to visualize my body spreading. I can think it, but I cannot visualize it.
It is very often the visual image of the body which hinders you from visualizing it. So it is better to close your eyes. Just visualize emptiness in a certain part of your body, for example, the knee which is very often contracted; see empty space. Then see how this visualization acts on the physical part. You feel immediately a separation in the lower part of your legs and an expanding. So, with the help of your representation, you can bring your knee, your leg, or other parts of your body to a certain position which is anatomically possible on the condition that you keep the sensation. But you must practice it.

Can one practice yoga too much?
When you love the piano you play it and do not feel it a chore, a "practice." If you are solicited to do the movements, do not refuse. But never let it become a habit. You will know it is a habit if you feel something is missing in your day when you have not "practiced."

What is love in life, how does it function, because sometimes it seems difficult and sometimes it is easy?
Before loving your surroundings, you must first love yourself. Not, of course, the image that you have of

yourself, but your real self. When you look at things from this higher principle which we call love, all things become lovable. Things appear constantly according to your point of view. Love must become your nearest. It is your nearest and also your dearest. Be in identity with it. In love there is no place for somebody. Love is not a state which you go in and out of. It is the principle which is our permanence.

More than death, of which I have no experience, I am afraid of illness, of which I have experience and which is also a kind of death in life. So the question is: How do I face this situation?

When you emphasize the illness, you become its accomplice. To understand and to know how to deal with it, you must come nearer to it. In other words, you must welcome it. In welcoming it, it tells you exactly its secret. But welcoming comes from the higher principle, from life. So emphasize life. The illness refers also to life. But in any case, only an object can be ill. Life can never be ill. In dealing in this way, you will see that all appears in your life, in your welcoming; all is in you, but you are not in it.

Dr. Klein, I would really like to love myself, but the self that I know now is the image that I have. So how can I get to know the real self, so that I can love it?

The real self is free from all representation, it is not objective. It is your nearest. You can find it in your stillness, in your openness. If you make it an object, you make a state of it. Our nearest is permanent, it is constant.

A very painful element in the relationships between people is when the one accuses the other. Why is there this situation? Has it got to do with the insecurity of the personality, and what can be done about it?
Who is accused? Find out.

How do I find it out?
First you are obliged to think it. If you do not think it, where is it? Being recognized, being loved, being accepted, being qualified, is all really a ridiculous business. Who is there to be recognized? Do not give any hold to it. As long as you identify yourself with the image, there is provocation. Just take yourself for nothing. When you take yourself for nothing, you are beautiful. You do not need to try to be beautiful.

In answer to a question yesterday about meditation with a mantra, I am not sure if I understood the answer, but I thought you said that one could meditate with a mantra. Could you say something more about this?
Saying a mantram needs right pronunciation and right pronunciation makes the body-mind tranquil, but still that is not really meditation. It still keeps the idea of a meditator alive. In meditating in this way, you are looking for a goal and you can never be free when looking for a result. Saying a mantram can never bring you to what I understand by meditation. For me, meditation is a

49

constant current of love. It is timeless. The mind cannot understand what is beyond the mind. It must give up and it gives up naturally when it sees its limits. Then there is no meditation from eight to nine or from six to seven; it is constant. It is the lively background in the presence of activity or in the absence of activity. It is not an introversion nor an extroversion, because there is no inside or outside. Introverted practices with closed eyes and no thoughts create states which you go into and out of. But continue to do it as long as you have not understood what you are doing—looking for a result. When you really see that you are looking for a result, you can give it up. There will be moments in life when there is a natural feeling of giving up, where there is not a voluntary giving up, but, rather, when life has spontaneously given it up. These are moments that are creative. Give your whole life to them. They belong to eternity, they do not belong to moments of space and time. It is like the love that you feel at a certain moment and you write a poem or you go to the piano and play an etude of Chopin. There is no intention in this, only loving the explosion.

All the yogis, even the Buddha, meditated in isolation and with closed eyes. This does not tally with what you are saying, and I cannot understand it.
The eyes, generally, are half-closed because the relaxed eyelids are very heavy. And sitting under a tree with your eyes closed does not mean that you are in meditation.

[Another questioner] How does our friend know that the

Buddha meditated with his eyes closed?

Sir, I have heard you talk of a kind of "shock" when the mind stops and there is a reorchestration of energy. Can you say something more about this and also about dealing with the residues of psychological memory?

Thinking is deploying energy. The mind becomes still the moment it is free from wrong thinking. By "wrong thinking" I mean the idea that there may be something to attain, to become, to achieve. This way of thinking keeps us in conflict, because all that we can find is objective. When we see this, the waste of energy expended in wrong thinking comes to a stop.

As long as there is an "I-concept," there is affectivity. Free from the "I-concept," there is no more affectivity. There is affection but not affectivity. Affectivity is a robber. It invades all situations and steals peace. You can only free yourself from the "I-concept" when you do not feed it. There comes a moment when you ignore it and forget it. It continues its function, but it is not you.

The way you invite us to experience life is the simplest and the easiest because it is the natural way, as you say. Many moments I live what you are saying, but then the mind comes in and says, "No, it can't be that easy," and then I am imprisoned in this game. So the question is, how to come out of it, what to do?

Dear friend, see it. In seeing it you are out of the game. There is nobody in the game. Remain in whole seeing. Be aware of the reflex to doubt. Ask immediately who doubts. It is a looking without the desire for a result, an innocent looking. There is a moment in which you do not emphasize the game, the prison, but you emphasize the looker. Have a real, non-objective relation with yourself. You will see that there is no self. And you will also see the surroundings from this non-objective looking. Then there is not a you and not another. In the absence of a you and another, there is really a love relationship. Conversation, living, dealing with things, immediately take a different shape, free from the self-image. A new quality of relationship comes. Otherwise, there is a constant "I want, I want, I want."

Jean, from what you've said, the body-work is really like meditation with an object. And the object is sensation. If we find that we drift off into conceptualizing in the body-work, I assume we come back to the sensation. And this process of being with pure perception, in this case sensation, has a quieting effect on physiology and the mind. What is the advantage of this kind of body-work meditation, as compared to the kind of meditation where someone sits quietly and instead of speaking the mantra, the mantra is thought very, very gently, very quietly within the mind. And the mantra is not being thought with concentration, but the awareness explores the subtle vibration of the mantra, the subtle impulses of the mantra. And if the mantra fades away, then gently the mantra is brought back. So the question is: As both are meditation with an object, what is the advantage (I assume there is an advantage) of the body-work over this other kind of meditation?

Every object refers to its perceiver. On the level of the mind, in the divided mind, there is an object and a perceiver. But on the level of functioning, there is not something perceived and a perceiver, there is simply perceiving. So every object can bring you back to your real nature. Your body is nothing else than sensation and sensation can bring you back to your real nature. All that is perceived in space and time has its homeground in consciousness; in other words, can bring us back to our nature. We said yesterday that it was said by Krishna Menon that every object can bring us back to our real nature. But in sitting down every morning and saying your mantram, there is, consciously or unconsciously, the intention to obtain a result. If you learn how to pronounce the mantram correctly, there is some pleasure, I agree, because, as we have already said, the mantram is sound vibration which acts on the brain. But when you sense your body, when you sense certain parts of your body, immediately this part which is sensed presents itself in certain vibrations. The postures affect the whole body, but the effect of the mantram is limited. There is only one mantram: "I am." There are no other mantrams.

You still emphasize the object, the subtle sensation. You must put all your emphasis on awareness, the subject which is empty of all qualification. In real meditation there is no doing. Doing is doing, and not-doing is doing, too. There is no doing.

There is doing in the body-work as well? I mean, we have

been "doing" the body-work.

Yes, I agree there is an apparent contradiction. But in the direct approach, you sometimes use things which are also used in the dualist system. The difference is that the ultimate is always the background; the accent is always on awareness. So, strictly speaking, teaching is non-teaching. Only in non-teaching is there direct teaching. In our quiet sitting we are not looking for a result. It is only for the love of sitting all together. It is very far to come here; otherwise, we would come every morning.

Thank you.

Let us be open to our dialogue.

I want to ask how to pray.
Praying is not asking. Inquire of yourself the motive for wanting to pray. Is it for asking, or is it for thanking? The highest thinking is praying. Thinking does not start from thinking. It begins with silence. This silence is prayer. Prayer is offering from nobody to no one.

In answer to my question yesterday about maturity, you said maturity comes through inquiring. Can you say something about this inquiry so that it is not a mental or intellectual activity?
Ask questions without any conclusion, without any reference to the person, to the "I-concept." Then wait for the answer. This brings you to ripeness, to growth. Ask about what has never changed in your life. Inquire. Ask yourself what is your nearest.

When we say "give up," is it doing nothing or is it doing something, and if so, what is it that we do?

Giving up is doing, it is giving up something. When you give up by will, you are looking for a result. There is still someone who is in becoming. Real giving up comes through understanding and understanding appears when the doer is absent from doing and not doing.

You have said, Dr. Klein, that we can forget the words which are said here, so my question is: If we are to forget them, why do we say the words?

The concept is not what it conceptualizes. "Sugar" is not sweet. The word is more or less a pointer. Live really with the perfume of the sayings; they bring you to what you desire.

Usually, we ask roughly the same things and we get roughly the same answers. What can change by hearing again the same thing?

One can hear the words from different angles, different directions. Ask what is the seventh direction. You will find it is not a direction. It points to your heart, from where all directions depart. Turn to the seventh direction. The saying must produce the understanding in you. Understanding can only come from the heart. You must make this understanding, this formulation, your own. What is said to you is the truth. Be open to it.

You once said that the girl on the streets of New York in the rain has more opportunity to really have a glimpse of truth

than the person who has all worldly comforts and no dark history. Is it true?
It is true because all his worldly goods furnish his mind and body so that he forgets his soul. Like the child in the toy shop who forgets his mother.

But is not the girl on the streets taken by her survival?
Yes, but with the rich man the forgetting is too strong, whereas the poor man may accept it and say, "It belongs to my life." Greed, becoming, is very powerful and remembering is weak. It is constantly postponed. But one day is the last day and you will be obliged to face the truth.

You must never postpone asking for truth. You must never postpone remembering the soul. If it comes to you in the street, better to be hit by a car than postpone it again! Then it is vitally important to remember your soul every day. It is a conscious recall.

What you just said about the furnishing of the wealthy man's mind reminds me of the beautiful story about Vishnu and the cow which I have heard you tell many times. Will you say it again for those who have not heard it?
Your English is better than mine, please tell the story.

I hope I can do it justice. Lord Vishnu one day decided to see how things were going amongst his devotees, and, taking a disciple with him he incarnated as a sadhu. He arrived at the gates of a great maharaja and asked for alms. The maharaja recognized him, was very generous and held a great banquet in his honor. At the end, Vishnu said, "Great King, you have been most generous. I would like to give you a gift. What do you most desire?" The maharaja said, "Oh Vishnu, you know the heart of mankind better than all, give me whatever will most please me." So Vishnu tripled his wealth and the king was overjoyed. Then Vishnu went on his way and some time later came to the hut of a poor farmer who was also a devotee. Vishnu begged for food and the poor man said, "I have only a cow, so I can only offer you milk, but please accept it from my heart." Vishnu drank the milk, thanked the man and asked him what he would like in return for the favor. The poor man said, "Oh Lord, you know far better than I do what I most desire." Vishnu left and, as he walked past the cow, it dropped dead. Further down the road the disciple of Vishnu who had been in great agitation since the cow died, burst out, "Master, I do not understand at all. You tripled the wealth of the maharaja and killed the cow of the poor man. Why?" "Because," said the great lord Vishnu, "the cow was all that stood between him and me." It is a most beautiful story.

Dr. Klein, a lot has been said about so-called meditation, how long in the morning, how long in the evening, etc., but you emphasize meditation 24 hours a day. Could you help us with some tools or techniques (if that is possible) which will help us with the 24-hour meditation?

During sleep you live in your glory. There is a moment when you are not really awake in the body, but you feel yourself in glory. You will discover in you what is continuous, what never stops. The discontinuity, thinking, perceiving, appears in this continuum. Most important is that you wake up in this continuity. But there is nobody to take note of it. You will know it without knowing it. In any case, do not try to make it objective. Let it come to you; do not try to meditate, do not try to go into meditation. You risk making a state of it. You must first have a glimpse, an insight of it, and then you will be solicited by it. It is waiting for you. My answer is only a stimulation for you. It is not a conclusion.

You said that It is waiting for us. With the usual method of prayer or meditation which is given by most teachers in the East, can we not send a message to It that we want to come near It and be It, be one with It, be united with It?
Why send a message? You are It. See only that you refuse it. You would like to sit on a chair when you are sitting on a chair.

But I do not understand that I am sitting on the chair. Could it be that with prayer or meditation I will understand it?
You will come to the understanding that all which is not "chair-sitting" is not you. See in you that which is not "chair-sitting." In other words, see what you are not. All that is an object is not you. That moment of seeing is from the perspective of what you are. You will find yourself, one moment, completely in this unity.

In our present condition, in our present state, we are not capable of knowing the truth really. We see relative truth and act upon it and a little later with more understanding we find that it is not the truth. When you say that we should follow the truth, is it what we see as the truth in the moment that we follow?

You are the truth in this moment, but you would like to see it objectively. It is what has never changed in you. Find out what is the same in you for three, ten, twenty, forty years.

Why does our mind not let us see the truth, why does it not let us enjoy the moment?

The less can never understand the more. The mind functions in space and time, but the truth is timeless. Your real nature is timeless; do not try to make it objective, do not say it is this or that.

If I cannot comprehend it with the mind, with what can I comprehend it?

It is not through the discriminating mind. Some call it *buddhi*, some call it higher reasoning, but it is none of these. Nobody knows, because there is no place for a knower. [laughter] It is *vidya vritti*: a way of reasoning that is only directed to the self. It is not having knowledge, but *being* the knowing.

I think I realize that nothing can exist except truth, goodness and love, but to put real truth into effect needs insight, which mostly I do not have.

Try once and sit there and be aware that you are constantly looking for something.

I have not understood what you mean by "truth."
Truth needs no proof; it is its own proof. *Alors*, do not look for proof.

Would you please say something about discipline? Thank you very much.
A disciplined mind is never a free mind and can never act spontaneously. A disciplined mind looks for results or a profit. Do do not confuse what we call "attention" with "discipline." Attention is open, it is not directed, it is multidimensional. It is not the discipline of "being attentive to" something as is so often proposed. You do not need discipline when you really love something. But you may need a certain rhythm. In the year we have the four seasons which appear according to a rhythm. All your cells, all the composition of your body, ask for rhythm. So discover the rhythm.

But can I, with a troubled mind, find the rhythm?
Absolutely, because the body asks for this rhythm. Do not believe the stupidity of certain doctors who say that one must wait till the body asks for food. You must keep to a rhythm. That brings you to health and also to freedom. See in your body how much sleep you need. Do not lie in your bed when sleep is over. No daydreaming; you waste all your energy daydreaming in bed. Get up and enjoy your silence; silence is waiting in your body. Go for a walk, eat, work. It is waiting for you, but you refuse it. When you see something which interests you, which has beauty, you are naturally attentive. When you

do something and you enjoy it, you are attentive. The musician who plays, who composes eight hours without stopping, may, from the outside, seem disciplined. But he enjoys his attention. The painter is not disciplined. When you enjoy what you are doing, spontaneously, there is attention.

Discipline is violence with the body. One must see the distinction in oneself between "attention" and "discipline." Attention is consciousness; discipline is mind.

You talked a little while ago about understanding. I want to ask: Does this understanding come through giving up?
In understanding there is nobody who has understood. Understanding can never come through what has been understood. Thinking can never start with thinking. Thinking is looking away from thinking. Understanding and thinking appear in silence. Understanding is instantaneous. It comes directly from what is understood. It never goes through the discriminating mind. When understanding is being understanding, the non-understanding has been completely absorbed by understanding. One must be completely impregnated by this understanding. Every movement you make towards it is a going away from understanding. Understanding is potential; it waits for actualization.

This understanding you just talked about, which is instantaneous—is it what you have called a "glimpse"?
Yes, or an insight.

Or "taking note"?
No, that is something else. There is no more taking note.
You are taken by certitude.

*What is the difference between "taking note" and the
"glimpse"?*
When there is a glimpse, we are taken by the whole. In
this glimpse we have the impression we are completely
absorbed. We are taken by certitude. But in "taking note"
we are back in the mind.

*In the condition in which we are, is that glimpse or insight
the nearest we can have to truth?*
You see yourself in a dark room and suddenly there is a
crack in the dark room and light comes in. What is
needed is that you follow the sensation, the feeling, of
this glimpse. Follow it. You can be sure you will be
solicited. In other words: You will be taken by it.

*What is the effect of this glimpse on our psychosomatic
organism and on the film?*
This insight immediately changes the chessboard. Because all things are situated from a new point of view,
which is not a point of view, but a globality. You can
never forget it because it is not memory. It is your being
and remembers you. It is itself which comes back to you.
But of course, making it precise: There is no you. You
will see things, you will do things, in a completely new
way. There may be certain residues from the past, but
you do not use them, they do not come into play any

more. A glimpse is a light in the dark room. It is self-knowledge, non-objective knowing.

Did you say "non-objective knowledge"?
Objective knowledge is what you learn in the university. It refers to objects. But we are speaking of self-knowledge, knowing oneself. One way to go is to detect in yourself what is your dearest. In your inquiry you may see what it is to be really free from yourself, free from objects. Live really the essence of your dearest. Enjoy your autonomy. But you must be serious, earnest, really concerned with your real being. Do not fall in the trap of compensations.

What do you mean when you say "trap of compensations"?
You do not have what you are looking for and you compensate. You get married, for example.

Or divorced. [laughter] By "compensation" do you mean trying to acquire more and more objects to fill up discontentment?
Yes. In reality, you are looking for objectless love. Do not fall into the trap of loving objects. Then you are bitten by the poisonous snake.

I am not going to. I am staying here.

The answer to the question, "What is the dearest to me?"— does it come spontaneously or is there some mind activity?
No. The mind is at rest. But the mind must know that

there are moments for it to take rest, so that it is open to what is beyond it. Then you will feel in identity with what you mean by dearest. When you live with objects, you live in separation, you are isolated. When you really live your nearest, there is no separation. One can say the nearest is being established in love.

Are you saying nearest or dearest?
The nearest is the dearest and the dearest is the nearest.

Is there a chief feature in each person which stands in the way of their maturity, and if so how can one get to know it and eliminate it?
Life is the teacher.

What do you think about astral travel? And about getting out of the body?
I do not know about it. I am very happy in this body. Why should I get out? [laughter]

People do it as a way of gaining experiences.
Experiences are compensations.

Do you mean that our everyday life is a compensation?
Yes.

Then we have to change our lives.
When you inquire about your real nature, compensation will no longer appeal to you and there is spontaneous change.

It has been said that many things are potential in us, but I do not know what I have to do in order to turn this potentiality into actuality. I have understood from what you say that I have to do nothing. So, what can be done?

I have not said that nothing is to be done, but your doing should be free from a doer, free from reference to the "I-concept." But I think that what is most potential in you is waiting urgently for actualization. It is your real nature. Let come up that which is looking for actualization. What do you think?

I would like this very much. This is the purpose, the aim.
It is purposeless.

I am sorry, it was a wrong expression. Something can be done; I expect that something will be done.
All will be done when you, as you, are absent. Otherwise, you live in boundaries and in compensations. What is the dearest gift that your friend can offer you? Do not give an answer. There is no answer.

I do not understand why there is no answer.
If there was an answer, it would make it objective.

Thank you.
If it were made objective, it would be like a box of Swiss chocolates.

And if that answer was "love," as you use the word . . .
Yes, the answer is love. But the word "love" is a very poor

word for love. When one says it, it lasts for three or four days. But real love remains forever.

Can you please talk about what you call the "double absence"?
It is the absence of the absence. I am quiet. This quiet still refers to non-quiet. So, take away the sound and the non-sound and you have the absence of the absence; then there is a marriage between quietness and not-quietness.

And this absence of the absence, this double absence, it just comes?
It is presence. It is always.

When this presence is there, where is the mind?
The mind is a tool. There can only be presence when there is *your* absence. Because this presence is totality where there is no place for an "I-concept." In the absence of yourself there is spontaneity. This presence is not objective. We can only be it, we can never think of it.

Thank you.

Wait in yourself for the question. It should not be a question that comes from book knowledge. The real question comes up spontaneously when you are still. Your question is heard in silence; the answer comes out from silence. So when you have heard the answer, do not come to a conclusion; simply let it be in you. Be aware how the answer acts on you, how you react to the answer. Let there be space between the question and the answer and the new question. You know that the dialogue concerns our real nature. It is what we call self-knowledge, knowing our self. I say "self"-knowledge because it does not deal with objects; what we are fundamentally is not an object.

So let us open our dialogue.

Please, I would like a couple of words on the self-knowledge of Jesus Christ's "I am" in contrast with the not-knowing of Socrates.

In self-knowledge there is nothing to know, because you

can never know what you are, you can only be what you are. So what you are fundamentally is not an object of knowledge. It is completely, absolutely, self-knowing, without any intermediary. The "I am" is an instantaneous upcoming. It is an apperception, an intuition. We are available to this non-experience when there is not an experiencer. We can never go to it, because there is no way to go to it and nobody to go there. We can only wait for it, welcoming it. This self-knowledge has nothing to do with thinking. When you are ready, when you are ripe, the "I am" comes to you because it is already waiting for you.

I have been to several of your meetings and, although I am fascinated by what you say, I find there are no questions coming up in me.
You are too passive. You are accepting the words here but not inquiring as to their truth or untruth in your case. This teaching must become your own.

But you also tell us not to think about the talks and now you ask me to think.
Yes, the sayings should stimulate the mind till it is clear enough to see what is beyond it. Be more active in the hearing, in the receiving. Let the essence, the perfume work on you. Do not refuse it, but listen to its echo in you. Let your attention be bi-polar. It is not the verbalizations you should remember, but their impact. Because the impact is you. It is only when you are impregnated that you come to a way of listening that is completely

different. It really acts on you.

Live according to the understanding. And as you cannot live according to what you do not know, see only that you do not live according to the understanding. That brings a transformation.

My question concerns everyday practical life. I want to ask what my attitude should be towards what I call ingratitude or injustice?
Every day is a new day. In life there is no repetition. So, face life with an open mind free from intention, because where there is intention there is tension. In tension, life cannot express itself in your body-mind. When there is reaction, ask yourself: Who reacts? When you look at life, look at it from your complete innocence. By "innocence" I mean free from any ideas. Look around you with your own light, not from memory, not from the past. Inquire in you what is the most joyful for you; be one with it, and face all your surroundings, all your fellowships with this joyful feeling. Then life is joyful, and your fellow is stimulated in joy.

Many times it is not clear whether it is action or reaction.
When you look at things from the point of view of the "I-image," from the "I-concept," there is reaction in one way or another. Most of our actions are reactions. Pure action comes out of right seeing, that is, not seeing through the "I-image," but seeing from whole seeing. This pure action is instantaneous; it does not go through the discriminating mind. There is spontaneity, and it is

adequate, right, to the situation. An action which comes out of this attitude should never be put into question.

What we generally call "instinct" or "instinctual behavior," is that another way of saying what you have just described?
Instincts come from body-identification, from conditioning. But in spontaneity you have the feeling that the body is in you, but you are not in the body. So you should acquaint yourself with this choiceless looking. When there is need to walk, you use your legs. When there are moments when you have nothing to think, why think? Our brain is mainly employed in daydreaming. We are closed in a vicious circle of choosing, where our mind is never free, is never empty, is never available. Be more and more acquainted with observation. See that you mainly do not observe, you observe through memory. Make it an observation free from thinking, conceptualization. When your looking becomes free from interpretation, justification and conceptualization, then you are open without any conclusion and things appear in your mind that you never saw before. The "I-concept" looks constantly for conclusions because it can only find a hold in conclusions. See how you function in daily life. Of course, at first you will see it only *after* the event, but still you see it—that is enough. Take note of it.

When you have a desire which is in conflict with social norms, or even with religious norms, what do you do?
In any case, free yourself from all beliefs, all norms. See that you live completely with beliefs. Free yourself from

second-hand information. See in you clearly what is beautiful. All that is beautiful in you is right. Look at the situation with an open mind, free from hearsay. The solution is in the situation. So, see the situation clearly with an open mind. Then the choiceless decision comes.

How can I avoid choosing in the practical, everyday things of life?
When you are free from the "I-image," there is no choice. There is instantaneous looking, whole looking, global looking. Look at things free from reference to yourself. There is no "yourself."

This global seeing, won't it happen through the mind, though? I find that I do it with the mind.
Do not make it thinkable. Make it seeing, hearing, touching, smelling, tasting. Let it come to you, do not grasp it. Your grasping is constantly looking for a result, looking for a profit. Let it come to you, let it unfold in you.

After such a beautiful and satisfying dialogue as we had last night, I found that as I walked out of here I suddenly snapped into my ordinary habits, not wishing to interfere or get in people's way. I'd like to know how one can retain the feeling and not suddenly snap back into ordinary behavior.
Change can only come through understanding. Let the understanding completely impregnate you. On the phenomenal level there will be residues which take time to eliminate themselves, but they eliminate themselves when you see them in the moment itself and do not go

into the old patterns. When you see something in the moment itself, you take the vigor away from the brain to maintain the pattern. The sudden understanding does not belong to the mind; it is timeless. The mind, as you know, can never change the mind; one thought can never change another thought. It needs a higher principle to change it, and this higher principle comes in when you are in a position of taking note. It is not an ordinary taking note; it is an instantaneous seeing.

When there is instantaneous seeing, which may be silence, is this silence able to articulate, or is the mind speaking the truth?
Truth can only be seen by truth. When there is instantaneous whole seeing or understanding, it is not an understanding from the reasoning mind. The mind sees a geometrical structure that makes you say, "I understood," but this understanding must become being understanding. In this being understanding all that has not been understood is completely absorbed by understanding and dissolves in silence.

The mind, though, has understood not what has happened but that something has happened.
Yes, something has happened. The mind understands it in space and time, but in whole understanding, space and time must dissolve in the timeless. The timeless is beyond the mind. So when the understanding is completely dissolved in being understanding, there is no energy, no pulsation to say, "I have understood." Saying "I have

understood" makes the understanding objective. A scientist who deals with objects has also the experience that when all the facts are gathered, there is a sudden understanding. But as he has to deal with objects, he says, "I have understood." The truth-seeker would never say, "I have understood," because he knows he would make the understanding, at that moment, into a subject-object relationship.

Is it possible that in our lives we have perceived this crack in the dark room that we were talking about yesterday, but because we were immature, we did not understand it?
I would say, potentially, yes, we are all disposed to have this experience. But the mind must come to its purity. By "purity" I mean free from wrong knowing. The mind must be informed that there is nothing to attain, to achieve, to become. This wrong knowledge shows that all that you can attain or become is an object in space and time. Recognizing wrong thinking for what it is, brings you to a state of alertness, of readiness. But we must live with our understanding and transpose it to daily life. Many people take note that they have understood, but do not transpose it to daily life. It is only in transposing it that you can really understand it, as a musician can only really say he has understood G-major when he is able to transpose it to B-minor.

The terms "Nirvana" or "Paradise," what do they define? Do they define states of perception, states of consciousness, states of being, or states of non-being?

75

The ultimate understanding is that there is not an independent entity, there is not a doer, there is only doing; there is not a thinker, there is only thinking; there is not a liver, there is only living, joyous living. In the absence of yourself there is nirvana. For you, nirvana is still a state, but nirvana is the absence of the absence.

And Paradise?
When there is no one to attain and nothing to attain, there is paradise.

I do not understand the reason for my existence and I cannot communicate with people around me, and this causes me great pain.
See how you have the idea that you have been born. You are the result of two people, but this is more or less an accident. You are only really born when you discover what is permanent, eternal, in you. That moment is your real birthday. Find out what is eternal in you, what belongs to the real birth. When you ask for the reason to live in this accidental birth, then I can only say it is to awake in the real birth. You must find love and joy in yourself, then you will find love and joy in your surroundings with other people.

How does this transposing of understanding to everyday life happen?
When we see how we never live in the now, how we live constantly in intention, in psychological time—past-future, past-future—and when we become aware of our

body, aware not only of its heaviness, its conditionings, but also that the energy of which our bodies are composed is constantly in a state of striving, that we are always in intention, in grasping, so that our tool is never ready for the unexpected; when we become aware of this striving energy, we feel ourselves to a certain extent out of the vicious circle of becoming. Then there is a stop, because there is no longer any complicity with this striving, becoming energy. On the mind level we have understood that there is nothing to attain, because we are "it" already, but still the body is in a pattern of striving. So it takes time to eliminate the residues. It is only in being aware of how we function that there is a transmutation, a transformation.

Dr. Klein, are the words of the teacher a description of the state that we are in but which we do not understand, or do they carry something other as well, for example, a taste of the thing, of the state itself?
The question is heard in silence, and the answer comes out of silence. So the answer is completely impregnated with silence for the questioner. The answer must be appropriate for the asker, and the disciple, the asker, must live with the answer, the sayings of the teacher. He must take the sayings and live with them without touching them with the already known. In this way they become his own.

Your own love and the love of the teacher are the same. When we say "love of the teacher," it is not of the *teacher*, of the person, but it is the love in the teacher that is the same as your love. And that produces the magic.

When you pronounce the word "I" there is no reference. The pronoun "I" can never become a thought. When you pronounce it, it refers to your real nature. It is a vertical feeling, a timeless feeling. It points directly to your heart. On this "I," we would like to have our dialogue this evening.

Sometimes you say the word "I" and sometimes you say, "I am." Why do you sometimes follow the word "I" with the word "am"?
When you say "I am," the "I" refers to itself. "Am" refers to the "I," and not to this or that. So, when you say "I am," it means "I am the I." Perhaps it would be easier to say "am," but the pronoun "I" is not thinkable. When you pronounce it in the right way, it makes you straight, free from time. When you say, "I am this," then the "I" is dissolved in "this," in time and space, in experience. But in reality what we are fundamentally can never be an object, an object in space and time. The word "I," when

it is used in the right way, is sacred. It refers directly to our heart. We automatically point to our heart when we say "I." It is so in all languages.

Dr. Klein, is it possible to talk of a quality of "witnessing" in this "I am"?
The "I" refers to our whole being, our global being. The "I" is not a fractional point of view, it is free from any points. When the "I" refers to our totality, then all that comes out is sacred. In this position there is no choice, what comes out of the heart region is right. So, one should not put in question all that comes out from this region.

What do you mean exactly when you say, "When the 'I' is pronounced correctly"? What is this right pronunciation?
"Pronounced correctly" means with no trace of qualifications. Then all that you are is included. It is your wholeness. All that you say refers to the "I," all that is potential is in the "I." So, all that flows out of the "I" is sacred.

When and how does the question "Who am I?" come from deep within?
It comes from the "I" itself. If there were not an "I," you would not be able to ask the question "Who am I?". So, when you pose the question "Who am I?", you can never find it, any more than the eye can see its own seeing. All that you can find is an object, a thought in space and time. But there is a moment when it gives itself up. It

must be a total giving up, and then the asker is the answer. It is our dearest, it is love. But we have said very often, one must be ripe, one must be ready to ask the question, "Who am I?". We can never go to the question. The question comes to us. We can only be in a welcoming state.

[young boy] You said earlier that we cannot question what comes from the heart. How do we know that it actually comes from the heart?
It is a secret feeling. In this moment there is no reference to anything about you. There is a feeling, a holy feeling. When you have discovered in your life something which for you is the dearest, you will not even confide it to your mother and father; you will keep it a secret. It is so warm, it gives you a fever. You forget that you are a young boy, you forget all that you know about you.

Sometimes, although I feel good, well and happy, my mind reacts with negative thoughts. Why this situation?
Make it clear for yourself that when you say, "I am happy," you are not happy, because you have made a state of it. In a state, you go in and you go out. So the mind is still involved in it. When a desired state has been attained in your life, you live in happiness, but there is a moment in this happiness where there is no cause and nobody is happy, there is only happiness. This causeless happiness is your real nature. Live it without finding a cause for it. When you give a cause there is anticipation of a repetition, which hinders the unexpected from com-

ing up. So, live this happiness without cause.

The "I" that you talked about, is it in my experience and I do not know it? Or is it in my experience and I give it some other name or some other cause?
It is not out or in; it is you, but you ignore it. The formulation of your question comes from the "I-image." You want it to be tangible, but it can never be objective. It is only through inquiring with an oriented mind that you can make it your own.

From where can the ego draw strength when we want to do something and we cannot?
It comes from your desire, but your desire is confused. You live your desire in ignorance. Do you really know what you desire? Is it to give security and pleasure to the woman in you?

I do not feel weak because I am a woman.
Are you *only* a woman? Why this restriction: to be a "woman"? Apart from the woman, inquire what you are. Why this fractional living? When the situation asks you to be a woman, then be a woman. But situations in life do not ask you to constantly be a woman. Free yourself from the woman. In any case, this country is a man's society—so free yourself from what this society has done to you.

What has it done to me?
A man's society emphasizes the woman, pushes you to

be a woman. It has put you in a cage. You are much, much more than the society has made of you. You are simply a being, a beautiful being. When you see the cage, it is enough. You do not need to try to escape from the cage. Then you belong to it, because, in trying to escape it, you are in complicity with it. See that only the seer is out of it.

A little while ago, you described a state in which there is complete lack of thought. These moments come to my mind always as the past, as what has happened. Can one do anything about this?
You make these moments a blank state, because you consider them an absence of thought. But at those moments there is the light of your real nature. All that is perceived is more or less a superimposition on what is constant, what is a continuum, what *is*. But you are accustomed only to living in relation to objects, in the subject-object relationship. For you, the blank state is the absence of thinking. But in reality the blank state is an object perceived and conceived in space and time. It has no existence in itself, it needs a perceiver. Who is the perceiver?

The few times that I have experienced absence of thought I have felt joy which has no cause, but I do not know how to have it more often.
Question what is the motive to think at certain moments. When life asks for thinking, think. But most of our thinking is wishful thinking, daydreaming. Be aware of

these moments of daydreaming. Just being aware sets you immediately outside the process. Then be your perceiving. It is only when you become aware of it very often that you become free from the reflex.

When you say, "Be aware," what meaning does it have? Is it up to me to be aware?
There are many moments when there is no reason, no vital need to think. Yet you furnish these moments with thinking because you feel a certain insecurity, or you are bored.

In the past you have spoken about letting the mind become exhausted. My mind is showing no sign whatsoever of fatigue in this game. Can you help me get my mind to go beyond itself?
The mind cannot go beyond itself through its own will. At a certain point it can no longer stay in the realm of thinking and there comes a moment when we find ourselves at the threshold of being. It is only a spontaneous giving up. You will find yourself open, in a state of waiting without waiting. Then you will be open to the openness. But this is not a process of will. What you are looking for can never be asserted, can never be objective, can never be affirmed—impossible! It is ultimate negativity. It is better to say, "I don't know." In this not-knowing there is real knowing. What you are ultimately can never be known, because there is no knower.

I do not understand what you mean by this "ultimate negativity."

The ultimate truth is openness. It has no frontier and it has no center. So, when you understand something objectively, it is not the ultimate. The ultimate can only appear in your total absence. Find the opportunity in your life to be in this total absence. It is only in this ultimate absence that there is presence. But in this presence there is no place for an "I-concept," for the person that you believe yourself to be. There is no more hold.

Is the absence of life deep sleep or death?
Deep sleep is the highest non-dual state that you can experience, but it is temporary. When you know life there is no place for death because you are in your continuum. So, remain in life and death has no more meaning.

You explained before that we are not aware during everyday life. The question is: Do we actually have a say in being aware or not being aware? Is it a choice we have, to be or not to be aware?
To be or not to be…[laughter]…*that* is the question. When you really live the question, then you see that you are beyond the "be" and the "not to be." So "being" and "not being" must disappear. Then there is being the being. Being and not-being refer to being. That being is beyond being and not-being. You see, this is the double absence of which we spoke yesterday.

Thank you for coming.

We are ready for our dialogue.

Dr. Klein, I am attending some courses, some lessons at a center whose main teaching is positive group meditation and the healing of illness based on the teaching of Alice Bailey. After a week of listening to you here, I feel that the group meditation is not useful because there is always a meditator and a goal to be achieved. I would like, please, for you to confirm that this is so, and also can you tell me about the second practice, the healing, if that is useful.

Meditation is not in space and time and one must be invited to meditate; otherwise, you are looking, more or less consciously, for a result. So you should continue your meditation until the moment that you clearly see there is no meditator and there is nothing to meditate on. In this stopping you do not give any more hold to thinking, then you remain in a state of stillness. In a state of stillness, there is nobody still and there is nothing to still.

As for the healing, I am not very well informed. I met Alice Bailey very many years ago in the Theosophical Society and I really do not know what this practice of healing is. But before you proceed with healing, you must first have discovered life in your own body. And then you can also stimulate life in another. The healing only has some virtue the moment you are completely free from the person.

[young boy] Dr. Klein, there are two kinds of meditation. One is to turn all your attention outwards and the other is to turn our attention inside. In your view, which is better? In subject-object relationship it is the same. You can only meditate on something outside. What you call "in" is also out. When you feel a weakness in a certain part of your body, it is an object outside. And when you see a tree or a flower, it is also outside. All is outside. There is nothing inside. Regarding what we call meditation, the best may be to fix yourself in your body. Sense the perception. You must be very innocent in your looking, in your meditation. Do not look for a result, for a profit. Then you will feel a certain distance between yourself and the object chosen for meditation. When you have understood, through your own experience, that the experiencer, as subject, keeps the object alive, then the observer becomes completely innocent and there is no goal or purpose. Then there is a fusion, I would say, between the observer and what you observe. This means that the observer has disappeared and the observed has disappeared also. What remains is only observing.

The best object is the body. But do not take yourself for a meditator. When you come out of the meditation, do not say, "I have meditated." The fact that you can say, "I have meditated," means that there was a witness to say that there was meditation. The real witness is not an object. So it is better to say, "I have been witness to the act of meditation."

Combining the two parts of the first question about meditation and healing, could you please talk to us about illness, and especially with reference to cancer as a phenomenon which shows great vitality with the rapid multiplying of cells.

All illness, and particularly cancer, is a reaction. A reaction to what? For example, there may at one time to be deep insecurity and this brings a strong reaction which can cause illness. Deep relaxation and visualization are two ways to face the cancer. You must face the cancerous part and visualize it completely open, visualize it in space, in expansion.

And live with your surroundings in lovingness.

This is a thought I would like to share, and perhaps it is not a question. After seven days of being here, many of the difficulties that I face in ordinary life have lost their weight, and my strength seems to be greater. I wonder, will it last when I go back?

You know the world appears according to your point of view, the point of view from which you are looking at it. When you look at it non-objectively, that means free from the person, free from the ego-concept, there is no weight, there is no affectivity. This way of looking at things and our surroundings is looking in love. When you go home, look again at your surroundings, at the life around you, from this point of view, which is not from the person. You will see things in a new way, because there are so many things you have not seen through your one-sided looking. In this new seeing many conflicts will dissolve. Things appear heavy when you see them from the point of view of the person.

What is the film?
The film plays on from moment to moment. But you, as the light which illuminates the film, are not in the film itself. As long as you do not see what you do in the film, that you live from the personal point of view, you are stuck to the screen. But actually you are the light, so be the light. When you do not look through the reference of your personal image, you are automatically the light.

Would you say something more about the deep relaxation and visualization used in illness, especially with reference to a fourteen-year-old child?
You can teach the child how to relax, how to be relaxed. If you lay him down on the ground, make him aware of the points of contact with the ground, so that he puts all his weight on the points of contact. It takes time to come to this letting go. All this must be done with closed eyes. When the eyes are open, it hinders you from coming to the expanded body, the relaxed body. And then you

proceed with radiation. You start from the global and go to the particular. First, pass over the whole body with your vibration, then you go to the particular point. You can do it with your hands. There, the tactile sensation is very strong and the light sensation is very strong. The best is not to touch the body. In certain circumstances it is better to touch the body, of course, but here, in this case, you should remain several inches over the body. You can also use this for self-healing. At the beginning, your radiation may be quite weak. It is in practicing, in doing it, that the life-body becomes more and more awake. What is important is that in healing the healer must disappear. The healer is simply a current, nothing else.

Every mother has this radiation?
Absolutely. When the child is very young one must touch the child. The child needs to be touched, to be caressed.

In self-healing can we ourselves touch the ill organ?
Yes. This radiation is much stronger than the radiation in the hospital.

I would like to ask how one can stand near a relative who has difficulties, how to stand by him without losing one's peace of mind. How can one help him?
Without thinking. Love him. When you love him there is no thinking and then your intuition will tell you what is to be done. I cannot tell you more than this. Love is the teacher.

I have something I do not understand. How is it that a great many teachers, who knew all about these techniques, died of cancer?
Some people think they have a clever answer: that the teacher has taken the cancer from others or has carried their karma. These are stupid sayings. The teacher is beyond the body. So, take away the "why," and ask from where comes the "why."

I would also like a clarification, please. What is happening right at this moment, Dr. Klein? In the silent lake of every-thing, the question falls like a pebble, creating a ripple. Then, after a while, silence returns, the answer comes out like a breeze, and at this point the answer is formulated to come out. Isn't that the fine point at which the answer can take a wrong expression?
It is in silence, in complete silence, in complete giving up, that our brain, all its cells begin to be regenerated. The real question comes out of silence, that is, from the answer. There is no question without an answer. In the end, the question *is* the answer. But in reality there is only one question. And the asker of this question *is* the answer. There are not two, there is only one. The only question is, "Who am I?".

You said before that meditation comes to you. What should the preparation be to welcome the meditation without get-ting involved in disciplines and practices?
Find out in you what is present, what has never changed. Meditation, as you know, is not a function. It is nothing

to do with the mind. The mind functions in space and time. Find out what is timeless in you. All that is perceived needs this timeless presence. All that exists is in this timeless presence. This timeless presence is not an activity, it is not a function; it is constant. So, being established in this current of life is meditation, which means being-in-meditation. But there are opportunities in daily life to be, without any effort, in this current, especially when the mind is open.

You talked a little while ago about illness being reaction. The first reactions seem to appear in childhood in the small conflicts between children and parents. Could you talk to us about this, and also about the relationship of small children and parents?

The appearance of a child comes from a very deep love relationship between the parents. So the harmony must be carefully conserved between husband and wife. The relations between husband and wife must be harmonious; otherwise, there is compulsion and the child feels it. This compulsion is very strong in certain couples and creates the roots of illness.

I am a teacher and I have to deal with small children. Most of them are hyper-energetic and the parents do not make the situation easier—even by the chairs they choose. In my relation with them I try to be quiet and I enjoy this. I want to ask if there is something more that I can do to establish quietness in children.

Arrange one day every month to see the parents. If there

is something to change, to clarify, it must be clarified in the presence of the parents. Do not oppose the child; go with the child, and in this going, transformation is perceived. The child must become creative, must know how to look, how to see, how to understand. All that is artistic builds harmony in the child. So one should begin artistic activities very early.

Is there something I can do for my eyes to be open at every moment?
See only that you are not open. That is enough. It is only in seeing that you are not open that you become open. But when you open by will, you close. Your eyes will always be open when you are interested in things that you look at. When you become interested in things, you are naturally attentive. You do not need to concentrate, you are attentive. Look at beauty around you.

I would like to ask you about adolescence. What should my attitude to my teen-agers be, especially when the attitude of society around is very destructive, with television, mass-media, etc.
You should take them in charge with confidence and authority. Real authority does not come from the person but from truth, from the facts. True authority is not authoritarian. You must teach *how* to look, *how* to hear, not *what* to hear or *what* to look at. Then the child becomes alert. Part of becoming mature is to recognize what is exploration and what is compensation.

How do I teach this "how to look"? How do I do it?
You must constantly be an example. But do not try to be
an example. You are already an example. See clearly that
when you look at something, you at once name it "book"
and you do not see it any more. So, become unstuck from
the concept and explore the perception. There is no need
to think, there is only looking. All that happens is in
space. An object in itself has no reality. It becomes real
in its relation with other objects in space. See how one
object acts according to the other object. See the perspective of colors, how they appear, how the color gives itself
to perspective: far, very near? How the light caresses an
object; it is the light that makes an object into an object.
Otherwise, there is no object. And what is really neces-
sary is your own light, your seeing, your hearing.

*What is the "chessboard" that you sometimes say we can
change?*
All your habits, all your conclusions, all your patterns.
But you can only rearrange the board through the mind.
Real change begins with understanding. Real change is
the elimination of the chessboard.

Do you play the game without the board?
Yes! Without any reference.

Is there "good" and "evil" in the world?
"Good" for whom; "evil" for whom? What is "good" in
certain countries, in other countries is "evil." It is only
you who qualify it as "good" or "evil." You can never

95

describe goodness. Codified morality is not moral. Every moment has its own morality. Your question is more or less an escape. See that it is an escape. If you take your stand in your totality, the moment of non-judging, non-comparison, non-choice brings you to clarity. Be aware that you are lost again in objects. The deep desire is to be free, to be autonomous.

Sir, all your answers are given from the point of view of non-dualism. Is that the only point of view? And from the existing religions, are there any that are non-dualistic?
All the official religions are dualistic. But within these official religions, some have an esoteric understanding. In these esoteric parts, you can feel the appearance of non-duality. But what is important is to see the truth. Do not discuss other religions. See the truth. Make it clear in your mind, in the act of hearing, that there is not a hearer and nothing is heard. There is only hearing. On the level of the divided mind, there is a listener and something listened to. But in the act of listening, in the act of hearing, there is not a hearer and nothing is heard. Let it be very deeply clear in you that the looker who is looking for something *is* the something. The looker is what he is looking for. There is no more looking to the left or to the right, doing this, doing that; you come naturally to your quietness and there comes a new or-chestration of your energy. What is important is that you take a stand in your own quietness. See really what is your own. There is no "you," there is only quietness.

In this state of quietness, where there is only listening and seeing, where is the mind? I mean, is there a mental experience which later allows a description of that state? Or is it a metaphysical state? There is something that I do not understand here.

In quietness, nothing is quiet. All the directions have been explored. It is not a state, it is your real nature. There is not a knower, not a controller in this quietness. Activity occurs, thinking occurs, function continues without a controller. Presence can only *be* presence. Being presence means being free from subject-object relationship. There is nobody present and nothing is present; there is only presence. When you think of being presence, it is already in the past.

You say that our real nature is non-dualism. What comes in between, inside of us, and makes us believe that non-dualism is more beautiful, more real?

It is your own experience. When you say "I" and you say "I am," all is included in the "I am." There is not an observer, there is not a controller, there is not a middleman in it. You would like to see yourself as you look and see a tree or a flower. But this is absolutely impossible because you simply do not exist objectively. It brings you to a kind of tragedy at the end of your life: that you have taken yourself for something objective. To understand it takes a great insight. It is not a belief. The same with the problem of free will and karma: You cannot have a quick answer for it. You have the answer only after long meditation, long inquiring. You cannot become convinced through one answer. You can be convinced only in living it and inquiring into it. In inquiring, the answer comes to you, but it is not an answer like any other answer: It is a conviction, a certitude.

Have you any questions?

Dr. Klein, I would like you, please, to say something about those tears which—I am talking about my case—which come when I admire something, when I hear a beautiful piece of music, when I look at a beautiful painting, a sunset, when I have a lot of love for something, tears which are spontaneous and come—I don't know for what reason.
They are expressions of your emotions. It is not emotivity—they are emotion. You cannot change it—why change it?

Dr. Klein, I am a little confused about questions and answers. Where exactly does a question come from? Does it come from the film, in other words, from the mind, or from the white light? And why does it come? Also, why does each question have one answer, and why is the question "Who am I?" the only true and real question?
There is only one question. It is "Who am I?". And this

question comes directly from the answer. The other questions deal with objects, they have to do with knowledge. But we are concerned here with self-knowledge, self-knowing. As this question comes directly from the answer, you must wait for the question. It will appear in you when you are very concerned, very earnest. You must learn, in a certain way, to wait. Absolute availability to the answer comes in waiting, waiting without anticipation for something. And then make it clear in you, the waiting is what you are waiting for.

Could you tell us what is the world of a person who is blind, deaf and dumb in relation to the "I am" and to creation?
The blind or deaf person during his life will find another organ to perceive the world. The world, of course, is different when you do not see it, but it is still the world. Lack of sight does not hinder the blind man from becoming established in the self, in the real self. On the contrary. It is in this waiting, in this openness, that we are really open; we cannot do anything but be open, but we must be open knowingly. To be knowingly open means being open in the openness where there is no restriction. All that is objective abides in the openness. But this openness is not an object, an object perceived. It does not need a middleman to be perceived. It is its own perceiving.

In this openness are we one when our physical bodies are apart, we and you?
All appears in this openness, all is perceived by the

openness. We are speaking of openness, but we can speak of consciousness—it is the same. You are first aware of your body, your body is sense-perception. When your observation is innocent, free from end-gaining, the body comes to its deep relaxation. This relaxation is not the dead body, which is relaxed, too. This relaxed body opens itself to life; it is the life-body. When the body has given all its secrets to us, then it dissolves in openness. We can use our breathing to help the body dissolve in this openness. In the same way that we listen to the sensation of our body, we hear the coming and going of the breath. The breath becomes finer and finer, like the breath of a baby. And, at the end, we have the impression that the breathing moves on one point. Then we have the sensation that the feeling and the listening of the inhalation and exhalation is in consciousness, abides in consciousness. In this deep relaxation, there comes a natural switch-over, the energy is no longer on the perceived, but the energy is relaxed, abides in consciousness.

Will the body-work help in this? I just want a confirmation. You first become aware of the pulsation of your body, the moving of the vital energy; the pulsation of your brain becomes slower and slower. The body and the mind are one. You know this from many experiences, for example, when you are nervous or excited, your breathing is very short and agitated. When you become aware of this agitation and penetrate it with slow breathing, long exhalation, long inhalation, in a few minutes you will feel free from agitation.

During these moments of rapture, when the physiology is very quiet and the mind is silent and all objects appear in silence, including the mind, including thought, what is the reason, if there is a reason, why one becomes identified with objects once again? Is this identification with objects once again simply to do with lack of knowledge? Or is it due to some physiological impediment or abnormality in the system?

Memory, conditioning, is very strong in us. Take note that there is a space relation between the observing and the observed. You have the impression that all that is perceived is in you, but you are not in it. You are no longer stuck to it. It is the thinking mind which creates time, but your real nature is outside of time. When you are once established in your real nature, there is no longer any return.

The mind must be informed that there is something beyond. That is enough. The moment we take note of this profound tranquillity, we are invited again. But the mind must be informed or, in other words, the mind must be free from wrong thinking.

When the physical body dies, does this sense of presence remain in consciousness?

The physical body is energy, matter in movement. It has its duration, but we are not affected by it. What is important for us is that we go knowingly through the threshold. That is why, when we are near a person who is passing away, in a certain way we must pass away also. In passing away with him, we help him to give up. It is beautiful when somebody assists you, with his presence, to pass away, assists with all his love.

With his bodily presence?
Absolutely. You give up knowingly. There is a moment of union with the person who is passing away and your giving up. You will both find yourselves in complete nakedness. In this presence there is joy, there is love without emotivity.

Dr. Klein, why were we created to ask the only valid question, "Who am I?"
This birth is the only opportunity to be born knowingly, to have true birth. Otherwise, our phenomenal birth is a nuisance.

To whom is one's birth a nuisance?
To the nuisance itself. [laughter] It remains an accident, an accident between two people.

Should we love our parents as a law, or only if we really feel it?
You must love your mother.

Only the mother?
One must give the mother a special love. She gave up her own life for you, and gave her unconditional love.

My mother gave very little unconditional love.
Then she was not a mother. But do you really know? The ways of giving are often unseen, secret. The actual physical birth is already a total giving and the following three years. In all traditions motherhood is revered because of the sacrifice of the ego at certain times, when the mother is beyond the mother. It is very often not seen enough by the children.

How can one remain firmly in the state of "I am"? Which means that one has succeeded in going against those forces that hinder one and which are very strong.
You are the "I am." See simply what you are not. Otherwise, what you are is an object, is a thought.

You mention in one of your books that the whole universe has contributed to this bodily birth and I must consider myself very lucky for this. The question is: Why? To whom is this piece of luck given, this favor done? In other words, what was I before I was born?
You must understand this formulation on a certain level. It is the stone that helps the plant, it is the plant that gives help to be an animal, it is the animal that gives help to be a human being. They have given them the help to be and they have given us the help to be. And not only this world, the stars, the moon, the whole universe has given us the opportunity to be. So this universe asks for—I would not say, for recognition, but for thanking. Take it as it was said; take it as it is; do not go too deeply in a Darwinian idea!

*[young boy] Dr. Klein, is it true that we are not this body?
If it is true, what happens to us when this body dies?*
All that is perceived is not you. You are the perceiver.
The perceived is energy. When this energy has accomplished itself, then it joins the whole energy, the universal energy. But what you are has nothing to do with dying. When this energy has accomplished all that is to be accomplished, what remains is our total presence. This presence was particularized in a body, but when the body has accomplished what it had to accomplish, what remains is life. Life goes nowhere, it is not here nor there; it is. What you are profoundly, *that* I am. What I am profoundly, *that* you are. That is how we are deep friends. From where could friendship come?

*[young boy] But there is a certain philosophy that says that
this life could be used in another body. Is this true?*
Life expresses itself in *this* body, not in another body. Do not go along with philosophy. Make yourself free from all philosophy. Feel deeply in you, where life is. Each morning when you wake up, you create the world, you create each moment of the world.

*I have read in your books that there is a passage, a passing
over, from the state of presence to the openness. Could you,
please, say something more about this?*
Your question is not clear. One goes from the state of cloudiness to openness. Discover in you what is the dearest for you. Do not think of it intellectually. Rather, let your whole body be active in finding out. Follow the

discovery in the same way you would follow a shadow to its substance. It will bring you to the most enjoyable. Do this with love every day, then all your activity will become enjoyable.

London, England

———

See from where you ask a question: The seeker and the sought are one. It is important to keep this in your mind, not only in your mind but also in your feeling, sensation. It means the asker has nothing to find, for what we are fundamentally is not an object perceived in space and time. In asking the question you must be available to receive it. You must find yourself in a certain availability, in a state of receiving, a state of welcoming. In this welcoming state there is no waiting for anything; it is simply being open. It should be very clear for you that there is nothing to find, nothing to obtain; it is in waiting that you are waiting.

The welcoming waiting state is not a thought, because when thinking starts from thinking, it is memory. Thinking is only a defense of the ego. But in the waiting of which we are speaking, there is an absence of yourself. It is only in this absence that there is presence, not as an object, but as your totality; it is a feeling of globality, totality, of expansion.

This presence is the absence of what you are not. Presence is never to be found in a subject-object relationship. It is neither this nor that, it is nothing that we call objective.

This is the central point of your inquiry. Live in it without any conclusion, without any expectation, and you will feel a giving up, even on the body level. The letting-go is not a passive giving up, it is passive-active, passive in that the "I-concept" does not interfere, and active in that you are in alertness. You are waiting, being open. It does not come by will.

Have you any questions?

Dr. Klein, is the picture of reality that I have just something that I put together out of wishful thinking, or is there some sort of reality in it? I mean, it hurts when one runs up against a wall.

But you refer to *doing* when there is nothing to do. Only wait, only listen. The looker is what he is looking for. The perceiver is consciousness; there is nothing but consciousness. You can look at the world from many perspectives: when you look at it from the point of view of the body the world is only sense perception, from the mind there is only mind, but from consciousness all is consciousness.

Would I be wrong in thinking that consciousness is nothing?
Consciousness is nothing objective.

Is it empty?

110

It is empty of qualification. The quality of consciousness is that it is free from qualification. You can find it only in your stillness, in stillness when there is no reference to anything.

I suppose in thinking that way it could be anything . . .
You know yourself only in relation to objects, in relation to the image that you have created. You believe that you can see what you really are in the same way that you can see an object. If there is anything to do, it is to become more and more accustomed to silent observation free from all conceptualization. In this silent observation you are completely free from thinking, from judging, attaining and achieving. It is an innocent looking, a pure perceiving. In this silent observation there is no you or other. In a certain way, you need to cultivate silent observation. The first step is to see that you do not observe free from any conclusion.

Why am I afraid of what I call nothingness? Why does consciousness appear as something unknown, unfamiliar to me?
Through your way of living you have emphasized objects and it is objects which have given a hold to your "I-image." Several months ago, when you asked me the question in the same way, I said that it is only on the level of the split mind that there is subject-object. In the act of doing and the act of seeing and the act of hearing, there is only one; there is only seeing, hearing, touching. Then there is spontaneity. Consciousness is already your real

nature; it is not unfamiliar.

Dr. Klein, does that spontaneity come from the wellspring?
Spontaneity comes only when there is a total absence of
yourself. You know, perfectly well, moments of spontaneity where there is no you and no other, where there is
only acting. In the absence of you, of the ego, of calcula-
tive thinking, your acting is according to the situation,
appropriate to the circumstances. When you keep your
self-image, you can never be spontaneous. You can never
think spontaneity, you can never try to be spontaneous.

When there is observation without any intention,
observation such as you find in a child, then you act
according to the situation. When your body asks for
food, you give your body food; when you are thirsty, you
take water. It is not a problem because it does not go
through the discriminating mind. When you are free
from the self-image, you know it more and more, because
you simply take note of the facts of how you function.

*I am very troubled by the word compassion. I have asked so
many times and it seems that I still do not understand that
word.*
I would say that compassion is your real nature. Love is
compassion; in love there is one, there are not two or
three. When you find yourself in completeness, you are
free from any choice because choice comes from a
chooser. Free from a chooser you are free from like and
dislike and then there is compassion, love for another—if
we can still speak of another—because compassion

comes as the spontaneous result of understanding that there is not another.

Is this that we call love a universal force? Does it flow through one, or does it start up in one?
It flows through us, it is our beingness. When there is oneness there is happiness, there is affection. When there are two there is affectivity, that means defense. Understand clearly what I mean when I say that there is not another. It is in daily life that you discover that you do not act in oneness. Become more interested in how you act and how you feel, how you face your surroundings. Simply take note without judging. When you simply take note without going through the discriminating mind, it is a whole seeing.

In global seeing you find yourself completely out of the process. You see the whole picture. You *are* the whole picture; there is no choice. In this way of living, a new way of thinking and a new way of behaving appear. It is right observation which changes things. There is nobody who can make the change, only right observation, and right observation occurs when there is no reference.

It is only on the stage that you can have this discovery and be convinced. When you are at home in your kitchen, all things are perfect. It is in relation with other people and other situations that you will see whether you have really integrated the understanding. It is the seeing that completely modifies the chessboard. There is no one who sees, no one who changes.

Is it possible to act without memory?
First you see, and when the situation asks for acting, you act.

But we sometimes need to act from technical knowledge?
That belongs to learning. Of course, you need certain knowledge according to your occupation in daily life, but this knowledge has nothing to do with self-knowledge. Accumulative knowledge belongs to learning how to deal with objects in a right way. But here we are speaking of self-knowledge, self-knowing. It is this self-knowing that brings an absolutely right balance to our life. A thought, an object, can never change another object, another thought. The higher principle must come into our daily life. Only this brings a completely new perspective.

Would you talk a little more about why thinking is a defense? If so, what is it a defense against? Is it a defense against openness, emptiness, the space, that is so frightening?
It is a defense in the sense that the moment it comes up the "I-image" is not in security, so it defends itself. In the highest sense thinking is defending, but right thinking is not defending. Right thinking is silent observation where thought comes up spontaneously. Right thinking does not come from thinking, it comes from silence. When you come more and more to silent observation you can see how, in daily life, thinking starts from thinking.

Dr. Klein, how can one give up?

When you see in a most clear way that there is nothing to take. You cannot prevent yourself from taking, but you can see that there is nothing to take. You give up because there is nothing to take.

How do we reach that point of seeing that there is nothing to take?
Would you like to be in peace? Would you like to be free from affectivity, from a relationship with others on the object level? See that your relationship with others is only affectivity. Affectivity comes up when you take yourself for an independent entity whom you must constantly defend. One day you will see that this self-image brings you nothing but trouble. You know moments when you wake up in the morning and take your tea but there is nobody who takes tea; you make your toast but there is nobody who makes the toast; you know only that you have taken toast and tea and there is no problem. The moment you take yourself for a taker of tea there is a problem. There is no entity taking tea, there is only tea-taking.

If I am aware while eating, and thinking, "This is good marmalade" and "This is good tea," am I one with the object or in dualism?
When you eat it you are one with the taste, but you do not name it marmalade. It is a pure perception.

In reality, what you want is to be free from conflict. Become aware of what creates conflict. In our society there is no conflict *per se*. We create the conflict. Free from the person there is no conflict. I do not say there is nothing, of course not, but there is no conflict.

Are you saying there is no conflict in society for which we are not responsible? Or are you saying that conflict only exists in our perception?
Conflict exists in the presence of the "I-image," but, as the "I-image" is a fabrication, conflict is also, in a certain way, a fabrication. When one lives free from the "I-image" one is no longer an accomplice to the conflict. Then you see the cause.

Human beings seem to have the gift of language. What is language?
Expressing oneself through symbols. The symbol is not what is symbolized. You use concepts, but when you take the concept for the actual thing symbolized, you are not always able to see where the concept points. The concept points to something. Before you use concepts, put youself in a situation of pure perception; observe birds, observe fish, without thinking, only see them, their shapes, colors, movements, their relation to other fish, without naming anything, only for the joy of observing. We are not too familiar with pure observation because as soon as an object appears to our senses, we immediately conceptualize it.

So conceptualizing is a misuse of language?
I did not say misuse, but we should use it in a less aggressive way. The conceptualization of a situation is

very often aggressive. There is nothing wrong with using concepts, but when you judge, compare, or condemn, you close the situation. There is nothing wrong with using concepts to explain the facts, but the moment we judge or compare, we close the situation.

What is left in you from the human side? I have not read any of your books and I do not know very much about you, but I am interested to know if any human aspects are left in you. I'll give you a reason why I ask the question: I had a very good friend who was close to J. Krishnamurti. I never met Krishnamurti, but my friend said that Krishnamurti sometimes got very angry with people and that quite intrigued me, that someone like Krishnamurti, who seemed to be very peaceful, would, in certain situations, be angry. So I wondered if you have certain characteristics like that.
Krishnamurti was never angry except when he sensed some stupidity. He had a very great talent for explaining adequately, using right words (not as I, always looking for the right words). He was content sometimes to be apparently violent—when, for example, he had explained "what is love" one hundred and twenty times, and then a nice person came up and said, "Sir, what is love?"

Isn't that still the human in him that gets angry even when someone asks a stupid question?
Sometimes reactions may appear violent, but this violence is something completely different. It does not come from the person. It comes from a feeling of justice.

117

When one thinks that some people are stupid and others are not, is that not judging?
Of course, if you say someone is stupid it is a qualification, but if they speak wrong words it hurts the nerves. When someone plays wrong notes on the piano it refers immediately to the right notes in you.

If one has an addiction of some kind which is detrimental to one's health, but one somehow can't discriminate, how would you suggest that one go about discriminating?
See the situation with your sensitivity, with your senses, without qualifying. The only way to clarify the situation is to sense it. We should come to see ourselves free from any objectivity, seeing, hearing, listening without reference to the idea that we have of ourselves. It is very beautiful to observe without qualification, because in this moment when our brain cells are completely open and free from memory, there is intelligence. In observing your neighbor free from judging and comparing, it is very interesting to see how love is created, how love comes up.

I think it was Plato or some other Greek philosopher who said that music refines the mind. If this is so, what effect do you think that so-called "pop music" has on people?
Music asks for the highest sensitivity. When you have this highest sensitivity you are already a beautiful human being. You cannot be a beautiful human being when you do not have this sensitivity to music. Shakespeare, in *The Merchant of Venice*, said it in a very brutal way but, still,

he was right: "The man that hath no music in himself...let no such man be trusted..." How does it go?

This is it, I believe:
   "The man that hath no music in himself
Nor is not mov'd with concord of sweet sounds,
is fit for treasons, stratagems and spoils;
the motions of his spirit are dull as night,
and his affections dark as Erebus:
Let no such man be trusted . . . ."
Yes, thank you. He said it beautifully, no? When you have not had the experience of music or painting or any other expression of art, it is the same as not having the experience of peace.

   Truth can only be understood by truth; truth can only be transmitted by truth. In silent observation there is only listening, there is only tactility, there is only seeing. Nothing is qualified. You become more and more aware of your resistances. We must learn how to sense our body. In silent observation there is not an observer, there is no one who criticizes, evaluates, compares; there is only listening. This is still in subject-object relationship—there is a listener and something listened to—but, as we become more and more familiar with this way of seeing ourselves, feeling ourselves, then we feel ourselves *in* seeing; we *are* the seeing, we *are* the listening, because listening is consciousness.

What is trusting? Is it psychological, a part of the discriminating mind?

When you do not trust, you should be something else, but not a human being. Trusting is the first quality of the human being, trusting your neighbor is beautiful, trusting is not calculation. When the lover distrusts the beloved, what has that to do with love? You trust the other one because you love him; when you do not trust him you do not love him. I take the word trusting as an expression of the heart, not an expression of the mind.

Dr. Klein, it seems the image we have of ourselves robs us of the chance to act spontaneously. When the mind is forming in the child and the image is beginning to form, why do we lose this spontaneity as we grow up? Why don't we keep the spontaneity of the child?

I have been waiting for another question from you. This "why" comes from the person, the "I," the "me." Can you not formulate your question another way? One should never give an answer to the "why."

The child refers everything to the context of the family, his acting, thinking, feeling, trusting. The child needs this observation; this accumulation makes him knowing. So when you are with a child you must watch how you behave, how you think, how you act, for, initially, the child has no reference other than you as a father or a mother. When you trust your child your child trusts you, you can be sure. When a child acts he never thinks in a calculating way, for profit. The relationship in our society is from object to object, man to woman, adult to child. In this object relationship there is only looking for security, looking to be recognized, to be loved. In relationships in our society the "I-concept" must be completely eliminated; then there is love, then there is trusting. See how you function in these moments when life asks for trusting, when life asks for loving, when life asks for help.

May we be silent together for a few moments.

Thank you.

The desire for permanent peace comes out of the experience we have in deep sleep. This experience is absolutely causeless, objectless, free from subject and object, and leaves a residue in us that asks for fulfillment. The idea that there is a cause for peace comes from our conditioned belief that objects bring contentment. But when the desired object is attained, there is a moment without cause when there is no "I" and no object. It is *after* the experience that we attribute the joy to a cause. In looking deeply, you will see that it is causeless, a timeless moment, a moment that is a window onto our true nature. The moment we say, "I am peaceful," we have made a state of it, a state where we go in and come out.

You cannot produce peace by will, you can only be available for it, open to it. What does it mean exactly, to be open, available? Generally, when we speak of being available, or open, we mean we are open *to* something, available *for* something, but here we are available for the availability itself. We do not emphasize the object to which we are available but the subject state of availability. We are open to the openness, which is not an object. It is what it says it is: open, unfurnished, free from expecting, anticipating, end-gaining. Here, we are completely free from the becoming process, because all is attained that can be attained.

This is just information to show you the perspective of what we are speaking about here. We should become more aware, more interested in how we function, and I think that it is especially in the night, in deep sleep, that the real gold is available. We should go into deep sleep with sacred feet, letting go of all kinds of qualifications, especially all kinds of affectivity. As long as we take ourselves as a separate, independent entity, we function in relationship of object to object and there is an accumulation of resistance and aggression. In giving up all qualifications in the evening before going to sleep, in going to sleep in our utter nakedness, we are open to a very important happening: Before the body wakes up in the morning there is a certain kind of awakening, not in the body, but, I would say, a kind of awakening in the peace, the joy itself. You will be completely awake in this feeling and should consciously take it with you during the day. It will help bring you to a non-objective relationship with yourself where, in daily life, there is only pure seeing, pure listening, pure touching and so on.

Then we see what we are really, the real facts free from wishful thinking. It is an instantaneous seeing without going through the discriminating mind. In this

clear seeing without qualification there is transformation. It is only this higher principle, what we call consciousness—and pure seeing and hearing is
consciousness—which can bring change, and what we
call being appropriate in every moment in our life,
adequate in every situation.

You have certainly something to say about it.

*Dr. Klein, you mentioned finding peace in deep sleep. Is
there a flavor of that peace which one may recognize during
one's waking hours?*
When the body wakes up in the morning you attribute
this flavor to the body and you ignore your highest self
which is the source of the flavor. You attribute this flavor
to the relaxed body. A relaxed body in the morning is
already something, but it is only a very poor residue of
what you really can have in the morning. So, we must
direct our attention, on the level of feeling sensation, to
this higher principle. The experience without an experiencer brings you to the desire to be one with the
stillness, to meditate. Without deep sleep, you would
never come to the idea of being alone in meditation.

*Dr. Klein, you speak of peace and you say that it is not a
thing you can get by will and that one has to be open to it.
The world is constantly seeking peace, and the world at the
moment is in turmoil. What are we, as members of that
world seeking that peace, to do about it, to find peace for the
rest of the world?*
See first that you are the world, that without you there

is no world. Look into yourself profoundly to see from where conflict arises. Your conflict is the conflict of the world. The world is in you and when you come to this understanding you will behave in another way.

I think most of us come here because we think that there is some key you can give us. Of course, any idea about a key presupposes the idea of being in chains. I realize that there is nothing I can do except to be open to the openness, which, for me, means that there is nothing to do. I see that my coming here tonight is a sort of deep-seated looking for this key of which I know there is no such thing. I'm sorry if it sounds confused, but I hope I am making myself clear.

See, in the moment itself, how many keys you are looking for to get out of the cage in which you find yourself. You will use all your wings to try to get out of the cage, but there is a moment when you see that you are constantly looking for keys and using your wings constantly and you will become aware that this effort belongs to the cage—then what happens?

The cage is the key, the key is the cage?

You want to get out of the cage, but the wanting to get out belongs to the cage. The moment that you see that you belong to the cage, you find yourself outside the process. And when you feel yourself out of the cage, look, look again.

It happens very quickly, it's like a flash. I feel myself out of it and then I'm back in the cage again.

Who is in the cage? Who? Do not give me an answer, I am not waiting for an answer. When you see that nobody is in or out of the cage, then you are really free from bondage.

This somebody in the cage and somebody out of the cage does not exist; it's an idea in the mind.

We find ourselves, as it were, tortured by products of the mind, and it seems that one reaches a stage where one recognizes that none of that matters, so one does not give it so much importance and one trusts that it will resolve itself. It is like moving from one realm to another where conflicts are resolved.
But there is no conflict. When you take a stand in your whole being, you are free from any object relationship, there is no conflict. It is "you" who create the conflict, for you still believe there is a "you."

Dr. Klein, can no object increase or decrease this joy, this peace? Is it constant?
It is timeless. And as it is timeless it has no increase or decrease.

But won't it be increased or decreased by an event?
That increase belongs to your psychology, but what is timeless is your real nature. When you first have the insight, you have it forever and it is ever new.

Could you tell us something about sickness and healing?
I know something about it, but I would not bring our

session here to this level. I respect it, but I think that the question is not completely organic, that is, adequate to the level at which we are speaking now. Would you excuse me, we may well come to it later.

Could you speak a little more about the type of relationship we should have with ourselves?
You are the result of two people, your education, your language, your surroundings and so on. A wealth of second-hand knowledge has given you a certain image and when you say, "I am this," you identify yourself with this image. Every time you look at a flower, or you look at a tree or a child, or face a situation in your life, it is the self-image that looks and everything refers to this image that you have of yourself. So, my advice is: Free yourself from the self-image, be nothing.

When you are nothing and no longer refer yourself to all this knowledge, you will see the world and your neighbor in a completely different light. Conflict comes into our society only because of the reference to the self-image. In freedom from the self-image there is not a you and not another. Then, relationship is healthy; it belongs to love and there is no conflict. I do not say there is nothing, but there is no conflict. In other words, free yourself from what society has done with you, has given you.

Twice you have said, "I do not say there is nothing, but there is no conflict." If there is not nothing, what is there?
There are events but they are naked, presented in a

factual way to you. Conflict is only for the "I-image," it exists when there is reaction. If you witness a situation that calls for action, free from reaction, you act most intelligently.

Dr. Klein, the word peace comes as the opposite of war. Does that mean that we have to experience our internal wars before we are in a position to actually experience this peace? What I am really asking is whether children experience that peace or do they have to go through the wars of adulthood beforehand?

First, see how you are continually at war with yourself. You direct your behavior in a kind of discipline and this means you are constantly in a conflict with yourself. You must first become very clear what it means to be in conflict. Who is in conflict? When you have to deal with children, you must be completely free from conflict. The child, in its first years, needs something to refer to. All education is based on imitation, so the child must see behavior very clearly. When you go deeper, you will see that there is nothing to educate, but there is something to direct, something to make the child aware of, to show the child *how* to look. But generally we never show the child how to look, instead we show him what to look at.

Can you say anything about the relationship between thought and feeling? You said last night that thoughts can arise from the peace, or they can arise from other thoughts. Can you say where feelings come into this, for it seems that impressions create feelings which then create many, many

*thoughts from other thoughts? Can you say anything about
this mechanism?*

Creative thinking does not start with thinking. When
thinking starts from thinking, it is, as we said, an aggression, a defense. But when thinking starts in silence it is
intelligence because our brain is no longer furnished
with the past, with memory. Therefore, it is fresh thinking. But, to come to a certain vision of thinking, one must
be aware of the power, the energy, that we use in thinking
and language. We use symbols, but the symbol is not
what it symbolizes; the word sugar is not sweet.

*What is the energy that you say powers our thinking? It
seems that this can be negative emotion, or it can be peace.*

There is not good or bad energy, there is only energy. It
is the thinking which gives you the direction, not the
energy. Thinking is a beautiful thing, but it takes time to
become really aware of what the motive is when thought
arises. Creative thinking is thanking, as Heidegger said.

*There are moments in my own life where creative thinking,
or creative doing, actually takes place, and my question is,
why does it not come into the whole of what I do? When
creative thinking happens, what a joy that is, but why does
it not flower and populate other areas of my life?*

Because you take yourself for a thinker, and you take
yourself for a doer. But where is the doer, where is the
thinker? When you come to the understanding that there
is not a doer or a thinker, then there is unfolding.
Thousands and thousands of books have been written,

but no one has ever written a book.

Could I say then that what I am doing is really looking back on something where I was not?
Yes. After the doing you say, "I have done it."

And that is the reason why it does not happen in other areas of my life.
You could perhaps say, in another way, "I have been a witness to it, because I can remember that I acted this way," but you should not objectify that you are the doer. Then you will see the unfolding.

The doing without a doer is so completely fulfilling, why does it not move "me" out of the way twenty-four hours of the day?
When something has been done and you say to yourself, "I have done it," see what happens in this moment. It stops the spontaneous doing. You interrupt the creativity of the doing.

Why do I do that?
I would like you to find out for yourself.

You talked about energy and you said that there was no good or bad in it. Isn't energy bad when it is linked with a desire for something?
There is only energy acting in different moments. When you die, energy goes to energy. To where moves the energy? Dying does not mean going somewhere.

But if I use my energy to satisfy some desire, isn't that bad? When I use my energy to get somewhere, when there is desire involved, when it is not simply used to cross the road, but towards some kind of state, or to desire an object, isn't that when the energy becomes bad and we lose the peace and experience stress?

All your energy is at your disposal. There is nobody who directs the energy. There is only energy-directing. You believe that you direct the energy.

Yes, yes, I do.

You believe that you direct your life as you want it to be; you *believe* it. Did you ask to be born? Will you ask to die? Have you asked for the suffering that you have had in the past years?

Perhaps I have, yes, it has come from me.

My intervention is only to stimulate you. I will give you no answer. But think it out concerning the question of free will and karma.

So, if I have no will, I could have this peace all the time? If I don't consciously direct my energy, do I let it find its own way?

If I say to you there is neither karma nor free will, will that stop you thinking about it? But you may not come back any more! [laughter]

Dr. Klein, this lady says she desires peace. Should not there be only one motive, which is truth?

There must not be a desire that there is peace; you must behave really in peace. When you behave really in peace, then you create peace.

Dr. Klein, we have been talking about peace, we are all saying we want to find this peace in ourselves, and sometimes it seems that this is very self-indulgent. My question is: Does it matter that we are not concerned about peace in the world? Does it matter that half the world is starving? Is that important, or is it sufficient to find peace for ourselves?
You do not live as independently from the world as you think. You belong profoundly to the world; you are the world. When there is a part of the world starving, in a certain way it belongs also to you. You can never say, "It does not concern me, it is not in my country." The world is in you; you are the world. You have also contributed to a world which is starving.

Then how do I contribute to them not starving?
When you see that you have also contributed to this kind of society—and you see it very clearly—something may happen. Not that you become a professional do-gooder, but something definitely will happen. It depends on you and it is waiting for you.

Dr. Klein, earlier you mentioned transmutation as something that happens, a change in our consciousness. Is that a permanent condition, or is it something that we go into and come out of?
You know that you are conditioned by language, endo-

crine glands, education, experience; that you know. But do not think about it. Be only your real self. Look at what you are not without any interference; you cannot change it, but do not identify yourself with it—that is the problem.

Dr. Klein, would you please talk some more about letting go?
We can only come to talk about letting go when we become aware of all the zones which are in tension—resistance, fear, anxiety. All these zones must be sensed. When you sense these zones there is not a sensor, there is simply being aware, simply seeing without directing any attention. This pure seeing puts no emphasis on the objects and as it gives them no more fuel, you will soon see that you free your body in this way.

Reactions are very deeply rooted in us and should be sensed very often in daily life. As we have an organic memory of the natural, relaxed—the original—body, we can let go of these tensions and live in a kind of ground which is completely harmonious and appropriate to our actions. When you see that you are in tension, in reaction—which means contraction—see it without the slightest idea of changing it; just take note of it. When I say to take note, it means that the mind is not engaged;

it is whole seeing, it is being aware. Then the ground will become your body.

We can never have two thoughts together; we can never have hearing and smelling or touching and tasting simultaneously. We have an idea that we can, because it happens very fast. When we go to the opera and we see the dancer and hear the music, it appears to us simultaneously, but our perception is not simultaneous, it is consecutive.

Is there ever a danger of becoming too sensitive, of being too open or too vulnerable?
I do not see what you mean: what kind of danger?

Our minds being very sensitive might cause problems for us physically?
The more the body becomes sensitive the more the body is free. A sensitive body is the real body, the real tool.

Dr..Klein, could you say something about grace?
All that comes to you unexpectedly is grace. What comes from the mind is not grace. Grace is all, but you must be open to it. Our brain is more or less furnished to maintain the "I-image," but the moment you realize that this "I-image" has no existence, that it is only a thought, the brain cells are open to the ultimate, to the all, to the cosmos. And grace comes to you from the ultimate, the all-possible.

What is the purpose of resistance?

The purpose of resistance is to maintain the "I-image" with which you identify. But you must see it. And not merely see it, but see how the seeing acts on you. In all situations in your life you maintain this "Mr. Smith" that you believe yourself to be. You constantly refer to "Mr. Smith" who, in actuality, has no existence, who is accumulated memory. At the age that you are now, there are many years during which you have referred to yourself as "Mr. Smith." It is not impossible that one day soon you will see this nonsense very clearly.

I read in one of your books that at death the "I-image" disappears. Is that so?
All that is perceived in your life is nothing other than energy, and this energy will one day join the universal energy.

What then is the purpose of this life and death?
Life has no purpose. There is no purpose in life, because there is no one who lives and no one who dies. All these kinds of ideas hinder you from being yourself.

Wouldn't the quickest way be suicide then?
Who would commit suicide? The suicider has no existence. It is important at your age to realize that there is not a liver and not a die-er. Never think of someone who dies. It is nonsense. Free yourself from the "one." Ignore it completely. There is only living, and this living has been happening for many, many thousands of millions of years. There is not a special life for you; there is only

137

life. So when you go deeply into the meaning of life you will see that dying has no meaning. I think you are old enough now to inquire what is life, what has never changed in you. It is only when you discover what is constant in you that you come to the understanding of what is life.

Dr. Klein, can we say that we seek that which does not exist and therefore we seek purpose in life because in fact it does not exist?
What is the motive in you which brings you to think? Why can you not be still? Why must you constantly be thinking? You are not familiar with living free from objects; you constantly hold onto existence. See the beauty of being free from objects. Live really in vacuity. When life asks for thinking, think. And when life asks for acting, act. This simplicity does not come through discipline, it comes through understanding. So many books have been written about stillness, but real stillness free from objects comes through understanding, and this understanding is being understanding. You must *be* the understanding. It must not be detached from you as an object.

You say we must be understanding, we must be open, we must really see in order to know who we really are, but we can't deliberately be or do any of those things, and you say it is not a matter of discipline. I know that one can prepare oneself by meditation, by silence, by eating the right food and doing the right exercises, but these are all exercises of the will and of discipline. So it seems as though one is caught in a kind of "Catch-22" situation. Can you say how one can be understanding and be open without deliberately doing anything?

When you undertake something there is anticipation, there is end-gaining, and all that you can find is an object. On the phenomenal level there is no problem, but when you see that what you are can never be an object, you give up all disciplines, because in projecting a goal you can only go away from your real nature, what you are now. Knowing things in an accumulative way belongs to the progressive way. The progressive way brings us to the moment of a blank state, for the progressive way is constantly in subject-object relationship, and a state without objects is a blank object.

I am not saying there is nothing to do, but that there is no one *doing* anything. Only in the absence of the doer will you know what is to be done. Sometimes when one teaches the direct way, we employ certain elements that belong to the progressive way. This is completely right, but what is important is that in the direct way the emphasis is *never* on the object but always on the non-dual subject, the sensing, hearing, doing, being itself. In the direct teaching, understanding is instantaneous.

All that you are is the openness. You will find yourself one day in listening and hearing and looking. What you are can never be an object, can never be positive. When you go deeper you are ultimate negativity. But first we are, through conditioning, open to something and later we are open to the unfurnished openness.

In daily life, do not fix yourself on what is absent, what you do not have, what you are not. Emphasize only what you are, what you have in this stillness when you are completely alone. When you are completely alone you are not separate. See what is your own *par excellence*; it is your real self, it is your nearest. You can never find anything more near, nearer than your own self.

What place does gratitude have in this teaching?
I think thankfulness is there constantly, and this is thanking for being allowed to have the opportunity to be. To be a human being is something beautiful, rather than to be a snake! Our thankfulness should be constant. There is nobody to thank, of course.

It is the observer which maintains the observed in life, but when your observing becomes free from all intention it can no longer maintain the observed, the object, and, in this moment, the observer disappears and also the observed. One can speak of a fusion between the observer and the observed. To be in identity with this moment is meditation.

Any questions?

Dr. Klein, you speak about the fusion of the observer and the observed, yet you also say that we should not wish to achieve this, we must not make it an end-gaining. So, are we just to be aware that this is how it is and just be open and accept what comes?

When the observer is no longer looking for any profit and is empty, it is still. In this stillness it has no longer a role to play, it can no longer maintain the object and there is a fusion between the observer and the observed. From the point of view of the mind we can speak of an observer and something observed, but here, when there is not a construction from the mind, in this act of pure observation, there is not an observer and something observed, there is only stillness.

How important is it that the body is an object of observation? In a certain way, one can consider the body as a harp. Before you play the harp you must tune it. We must find the right posture in which the body can begin its playing so that it becomes the right tool in our possession. One can only feel, be aware of, this right position through our tactile sensation. It is our sensation which guides us to the right position. The body itself is nothing other than organic memory. So we can go knowingly into the right position of our body through this organic memory. When the body is still, the mind is still too. In stillness of body and mind, you find yourself at the threshold of your being. Then, you will find yourself in perfect availability, in welcoming.

Meister Eckhart wrote, "Of all of God's creations his greatest creation was that of stillness." Can you speak about that? The greatest creation takes place constantly. It is you who creates the world constantly. From the right point of view one can say that the creation is constantly, but there is not a creator, as there is not a thinker or a doer. It is only in the total absence of yourself that there is presence. This presence can never be objective.

Dr. Klein, I always thought that the sacred fire was needed

*and was an activity. Does one need the sacred fire and, if
so, how can we use it?*
Consciousness is not an activity, it is not a function. All
functions are perceived in consciousness, but consciousness is not affected by the process of perceiving in
creation.

*Is the sacred fire, the enormous desire to find the real love,
consciousness?*
When the truth has touched you, you are burning with
the desire for consciousness. There is no more duality,
there is oneness.

What exactly do you mean by the direct way?
The direct way is when we are touched directly without
interference with what we are not: body, senses and
mind. You may arrive at a moment when you feel a very
complete "I don't know." In this complete not-knowing
there is no reference to any of the known. You are
completely open. In this moment you wake up in awareness.

Sometimes one uses things which are employed in
the progressive way, but when you follow the progressive
way to its conclusion you come to an end where there
may be a kind of emptiness. But this emptiness is an
object too and you cannot come out of this relationship
of subject-object, this blank state. It causes a very great
crisis for somebody who has followed the progressive
way for years and years.

You said that the not-knowing was simply not referring to anything known. I have always conceived of this not-knowing as a blank state, but is not-knowing, then, other than a state?

Yes. A state refers to an object. Properly speaking, a state is something you go into and come out of. For example, we can face what is called in the language of Hinduism our "*Ishtamurti,*" that means an object which points to a very high feeling, a very high emotion—it could be Krishna or Vishnu. We look at this object, explore it, discover it, not only in its physical aspect but all that is behind it, and we come to a very high feeling of emotion. We can live in this emotion, we can even be in identity with this emotion, but still there comes a moment when we come out and then life can be dull. That is a state.

Our real being, our happiness, is not connected with an object. Happiness is really when you live with happiness, where there is nobody happy and no cause of the happiness. This happiness does not come to us in its naked state only because we have the deep conviction that happiness has a cause, and we continue to look for a cause. Thus we are constantly looking for a cause instead of being open, being in waiting.

Do you see? To look for a state is anticipation. A so-called object gave you satisfaction at some past time, but three or four years later when you saw it again, it did not have the same effect. Such is the way of all causes.

You spoke about stillness of body and mind as a condition or a state, a prerequisite for understanding. Can the mind

and the body be still and very active at the same time?
When you are still, there is no place for somebody who
can react.

I mean, does the body need to be static in order to be still?
But your real nature is still; consciousness is still. When
you explore your body in stillness, there is no qualification, no reference to anything; there is only pure listening, pure seeing, pure hearing. The nature of the body
and mind is not inactivity. They can stop functioning
from time to time, but to force this is violence. The
stillness we are speaking of is behind activity. Activity
occurs in the background of stillness.

*Dr. Klein, does that mean that when there is not pure seeing
or pure hearing we are in a state of conflict, because we do
not have this consciousness?*
Pure seeing, pure hearing or touching is consciousness.
The words "pure" and "impure" refer to the person.

*So, are you saying that as long as there is a person it will
always be in conflict, and it cannot be otherwise?*
In pure seeing, there is no interference of the person, of
a system, of a critic, of evaluation or comparison. The
discovery that when you look at an object, you can look
at it from many angles and simply take note, not conceptualize it, means that you have a moral relationship with
this object. The moment that you conceptualize it, you
make it impure.

How can we allow for our humanness?
It depends on what you understand by human beings. As long as you look at yourself from a point of view which is profoundly not human, you cannot speak of humanness. The image you have of yourself is not human. It is only when you free yourself completely from the idea of what you believe yourself to be that you will know what it means to be human.

Dr. Klein, since the mind cannot change the mind, could you talk to us about real acceptance?
Acceptance is a normal function of the relaxed brain. Before you see something, you feel yourself already in accepting. To understand something you must already accept it, and when you accept something—although you first emphasize what you accept—in the end you emphasize the accepting itself. You must be *in* the accepting.

But you must take accepting in the right meaning. It means letting things come, letting be. It is welcoming. You welcome all things as they come to you. In daily life, we are constantly solicited to welcome. In welcoming there is no discussion. Said in another way, we must love what comes to us. When you go deeply into the word "surrender," I think you will find what you would like to see in the word accepting. There is nothing fatalistic about it.

We divide things into beautiful and ugly, and we accept the beautiful and reject the ugly. Is accepting somehow tied in

with beauty, and the things that we call beautiful in this world, or is it a different sort of beauty?
It is an unconditional accepting. When you accept things you are free from the ego. In real accepting there is no place for the ego. When you accept things you accept adequacy. You are appropriate, you are adequate to what you accept. There is no discussion of wrong and right, of beautiful and ugly; you are free from the opposites.

Why is it, then, that beautiful things, such as a piece of music, move one to one's very being? And does that happen to one particular person and not to another?
Right spontaneous action flows out of the accepting, so let it become an experience for you. It may even not be experienced, but there may simply be the right understanding of what it means to accept. Accepting makes you whole, global.

Where does discrimination come in?
There is not a discriminator. The moment you accept something totally and you really see the facts, there is discrimination. But there is not a discriminator. The result is instantaneous, spontaneous, and should never be put into question. It is so, and not else. When you put it into question you are acting from the ego, the person, psychological survival. In the word accepting there may still be a residual taste of will. It should be simply a surrender.

When living in non-duality, how does one form relation-

ships, marriage partners and so on, or has this no place?
Mainly, our relationships are based on object to object,
personality to personality, man and woman, and so on.
On this level there is only conflict. See that what we call
"a woman" and what we call "a man" is a fraction, that
the personality is a fraction. How can you, from the point
of view of a fraction, understand something which is
whole, which is global? A woman must free herself from
the woman, and the man must free himself from being a
man. When we speak of the woman and when we speak
of the man, we have certain preconceptions. So we must
be free from the woman and free from the man. What
happens then? There is friendship, then there is love;
otherwise, there is not love; otherwise, there is conflict
on many levels.

*How does one know the difference between spontaneous
discrimination and personal reaction, or taste?*
Spontaneity is not in the world of thinking. It is the result
of seeing facts and acting according to the facts. Spontaneity is born of accepting the moment. Right action comes
from right seeing; reaction comes from fractional seeing.
And your reactions appear constantly according to the
stand that you are taking, whether it is with the mind or
the body. On the level of the man and woman relationship
there is only convention. If you take the stand of consciousness there is love and there is spontaneity.

*Does desire always emanate from the mind, or can it be
non-dual?*

Desire comes directly from what you desire. In your most intimate moments with yourself, see really, explore, what you desire. You will look in many directions and at the end you will see that what you once desired is now even hateful to you. So you come to the conclusion that an object can never bring you to what you desire. When you free yourself from objects, you will see that what you really desire is desireless. So, be this desirelessness.

About the object and desire: I find myself sometimes projecting desirability onto an object and then desiring the object because I have projected desirability on it—often an undesirable, terrible object that has no desire about it.
When you speak of a desire it is a concept, it refers to memory, but when you deeply inquire, you see that you are looking for a permanent state, for being permanently free from desire. This is disturbing, and you can only face it in your stillness when you really see what is permanent in you. Listen to it, and also to your reactions. The problem of desire is very deeply rooted in us. When we once have understood the perspective of non-desire, our nature will be completely changed.

If someone has been completely depressed for a very long time, is it so all that can be done is to welcome it, accept it, in openness? Or would it be an escape to take medicine for it?
You are too intelligent to be looking for medicine. Face it directly, but face first the sensation, the contraction, the resistance in your body. If you do not proceed in this

way, you will remain with the concept and this concept can bring you nowhere. When you feel in a melancholic state, an unfree state, see where it is localized in your body. Is it in your chest, your lumbar region or your shoulders? Explore it and with certitude you will come to where the melancholia, the unhappiness, is localized in your body in the form of contraction. That is the real place to begin to understand what it is to be unsatisfied. Make this part sensitive, make it feeling, sense it. In sensing it you come to a certain hierarchy of feeling and at the end you will see that the feeling frees you from the contraction. Do not remain with the concept, for the concept is only memory; it is not actual; the sensation is actual.

[pause]

In the last few days we have together shared and manipulated many ideas. When you take home the ideas you lose the perfume of these moments. But it is the perfume which holds the essence of the moment, of the sayings. Forget the ideas and keep the perfume. In many circumstances, consciously remember what you have lived here, what you have felt, what captured you. Let this feeling, without thought and idea, pervade you. Be it, without thinking it, and one day you will be it forever.

OTHER BOOKS BY JEAN KLEIN may be obtained from your local metaphysical bookstore or ordered directly from the Jean Klein Foundation, P.O. Box 2111, Santa Barbara, CA 93120 [805/963-5723]. Videos and tapes of conversations with Jean Klein, and information about his talks and seminars in the United States and Europe may also obtained by contacting the Foundation in Santa Barbara.

- *I Am* [Third Millennium Publications] $12.95
  Based on dialogues with students in Europe over a period of many months, this is a lucid exposition of Advaita in a vocabulary easily apprehended by the Westerner. 1989. 151 pp. ISBN #1-877769-19-3

- *Transmission of the Flame* [Third Millennium Publications] $14.95
  For the first time in print, Jean Klein discusses his experiences with his own teacher in India in the prologue of this book, followed by transcriptions of lively meetings with students in Holland, England, France and the United States. 1990. 304 pp. ISBN #1-877769-22-3

- *Open to the Unknown: Dialogues in Delphi* [Third Millennium Publications] $12.95
  Earnest students from all over the world gathered in Greece in 1991 to participate in a series of dialogues with Jean Klein. This book is the expanded text of those intense and illuminating discussions. 1992. 130 pp. ISBN #1-877769-18-5

- *Who Am I? The Sacred Quest* [Element Books] $13.95
  Unique among Jean Klein's works, the dialogues contained in this book have been organized by sub-

ject. Topics include: Relationship; The Nature of Thinking; The Art of Listening; A Conversation on Art, etc. 1988. 136 pp. ISBN #1-85230-029-9

- *Be Who You Are* [Element Books] $12.95
  One of the earliest books of dialogues with Jean Klein to be published, the French journal, *Etre,* said of it: "There is nothing to do, no one to perfect. This book explains this paradox." 1978. 88 pp. ISBN #1-85230-103-1

- *The Ease of Being* [Acorn Press] $9.95
  "Open anywhere, and one hears the music of mastery and the gentle authority of the accomplished." — *Mountain Path.* 1984. 80 pp. ISBN #1-89386-15-8

- *Blossoms in Silence* [Jean Klein Foundation]
  Signed, limited edition of Jean Klein's sayings accompanied by black & white drawings, 200 copies only. $500 donation to Jean Klein Foundation.

Jean Klein's books are also available in French, German, Spanish, Dutch, Italian, Greek and Hebrew.

Videos

- *Discovering the Current of Love* [with Lilias Folan] 60 min. 1989. $29.95

- *The Flame of Being* [with Michael Toms, New Dimensions Radio] 60 min. 1989. $29.95

- *Love and Marriage* [with Drs. Paul and Evelyn Moschetta] 47 min. 1991. $29.95

Audios

- *The Sacred Quest: Being Who You Are* [with Michael Toms, New Dimensions Radio] 60 min. 1989. $9.95

- *A Clear View: Vedanta for Westerners* [with Michael Toms, New Dimensions Radio] 60 min. 1987. $9.95

Journals

- *Listening* (U.S.A.)

- *Etre* (France)

- *Essere* (Italy)

- *Ser* (Spain)

Forthcoming

Living Truth by Jean Klein

A compilation of dialogues (including the pamphlet *Mount Madonna Dialogues, 1988*, now out of print) between Jean Klein and seekers after truth covering several years of meetings during the late 1980s at the Mount Madonna retreat center in the Santa Cruz Mountains of California. Scheduled for publication in October 1994.

LIVING TRUTH

JEAN KLEIN

Listening: The Voice of Jean Klein

The serious truth-seeker will also be interested in receiving the journal *Listening*, published twice each year by the Jean Klein Foundation and offered as a gift to donors to the Foundation of $50 or more annually. Personally edited by Jean Klein, he says, "The texts included in this journal are jewels of the highest wisdom…writings the most profound that humanity has produced."

Each issue contains:

- New articles by Jean Klein
- A classic text in the field of non-dualism
- Excerpts from talks or forthcoming books
- A section on Jean Klein's work with the body
- A question and answer section for students' inquiries
- Jean Klein's schedule of talks and seminars in the U.S. and Europe
- An update on publications

Readers also receive invitations to special small talks as well as an informal "Day of Listening" with Jean Klein some time during the year.

For more information or to make a donation, contact the Jean Klein Foundation, P.O. Box 2111, Santa Barbara, CA 93120.